Honoré de Balzac

Balzac in 1842
Daguerreotype by Nadar

Honoré de Balzac

A Biography

---

by

HERBERT J. HUNT

UNIVERSITY OF LONDON
THE ATHLONE PRESS
1957

Published by
THE ATHLONE PRESS
UNIVERSITY OF LONDON
at 2 Gower Street, London, W.C.1

Distributed by Constable & Co. Ltd.
12 Orange Street, London, W.C.2

Canada
University of Toronto Press

U.S.A.
John de Graff Inc.
31 East 10th Street,
New York, 3

Printed in Great Britain by
ROBERT MACLEHOSE AND CO LTD
GLASGOW

PREFACE

The worth of the 'Comédie Humaine' has been a matter for much disagreement in England, and that not only since the days of Balzac's admirers Oscar Wilde, George Moore, George Saintsbury and Henry James. His conception of the novel as a medium for social history, as the constructed fiction of an organizing and selecting mind, as an amalgam in which background-description, objective character-portrayal and logically-developed plot have their proportionate parts to play, set a standard until approximately the end of the first quarter of the present century. Since then it has diminished in prestige. Moreover his world is not our English world. His moral and sentimental values are no longer ours; indeed they have never been entirely ours. His compelling genius is offset by glaring and sometimes irritating defects. Yet he has his place among the world's greatest literary creators. Even in England his eclipse can never become entire or permanent.

In France he has scarcely ever suffered decline, although there was an element of the artificial in the publicity he received at the time of the centenary celebrations of 1950. In England he has been written about in recent years by such perceptive critics as Raymond Mortimer, V. S. Pritchett and W. Somerset Maugham.[1] In the United States he has been the subject not only of much scholarly research, notably in the University of Chicago,[2] but also of well-informed

[1] *Channel Packet*, 1942; *The Living Novel*, 1946; *Ten Novels and their Authors*, 1954. See H. O. Stutchbury, 'English Writers on Balzac', in *Adam*, June 1949.

[2] The great pioneer in this respect is W. H. Royce, whose *Balzac Bibliography* of 1928, admirable in its time, is in urgent need of being brought up-to-date.

analyses, like that of E. Preston Dargan[1] and the masterly appreciation of S. Rogers.[2] Nevertheless he has been, relatively speaking, neglected by writers using the English medium. There is no up-to-date life of Balzac in English, the most recent being those of Mary G. Sandars (1904, 1914), Frederick Lawton (1910) and Francis Gribble (1930). The first is a competent work, but now out-of-date. The other two, like many French biographies, especially René Benjamin's biographical romance *La prodigieuse Vie d'Honoré de Balzac* (1925), betray a strong tendency to linger over the sentimental, the sensational and the anecdotal.

Nor is there any systematic account of Balzac's Works which is at once historical, fully informative and critical. It has often been said that, for a complete understanding and appraisal of Balzac, a knowledge of the 'Comédie Humaine' in its length and breadth is necessary. This is a counsel of perfection, for few people have the time or the patience to work their way through, say, the thirty odd volumes of novels in the Conard edition.[3] There is therefore room for a study giving a consecutive view of the 'Comédie Humaine' from start to finish; not indeed in the order which Balzac's logic and, sixty-six years ago, Marcel Barrière's interpretation[4] imposed upon the novels, but in the order of their appearance in time, determined by the vicissitudes and caprices of Balzac's own creative activity. In the belief that it is still worth while for an Englishman to look at Balzac and see what he has still to offer to English readers, the present volume is offered as a biographical prelude to such an ac-

---

[1] *Honoré de Balzac. A Force of Nature*, Chicago, 1932.

[2] *Balzac and the Novel*, Univ. of Wisconsin Press, 1953.

[3] The complete edition, which includes Balzac's *Théâtre*, his *Contes drolatiques* and his *Œuvres diverses*, comprises forty octavo volumes.

[4] In *L'Œuvre de H. de B.*, *Étude littéraire et philosophique de la 'Comédie Humaine'*, 1890.

count of Balzac's writings: an undertaking which I hope to complete in due course.

Although—or perhaps because—Balzac's life was not sensationally eventful like that, for instance, of Arthur Rimbaud, it is not an easy one to set forth. Broadly speaking, it may be presented in two ways. The different aspects of his career and personality can be selected, and events fitted into the categories thus created. Unfortunately this makes for chronological confusion and blurs the sense of continuity— the biographies of Lawton and Gribble both suffer from this defect; nor is *La Vie privée de Balzac*, by Jules Bertaut (1950), beyond reproach on this score. Or a straightforward method of historical narration can be adopted, so that the phases of Balzac's life and his manifold literary activities may be more readily correlated by those who are interested to know what he was doing and how his affairs stood at any moment in his career. This volume tries to do this as far as possible, but without sacrificing the more picturesque features and without neglecting Balzac as a vivid and amusing person; for the story of a great writer's life and struggles has its own inherent interest.

The most important life of Balzac is that of André Billy[1]: a memorable one, but one whose bulk (two volumes and some 660 pages) renders it, not indeed indigestible, but too detailed for easy consumption. The most immediate sources for a biography of Balzac are to be found in his fairly extensive correspondence.[2] The rest has accumulated during a century of research to which Spoelberch de Lovenjoul and Marcel Bouteron have made the most monumental contribu-

[1] *Vie de Balzac*, Flammarion, 1943. Revised and enlarged in the edition of 1944.

[2] For example, *Letters to his Family* (W. S. Hastings); G. Hanotaux and G. Vicaire, *La Jeunesse de Balzac* (edition of 1921); *Correspondance avec Z. Carraud* (M. Bouteron); *Lettres à l'Etrangère* (M. Bouteron, 4 vols.; a fifth is being prepared by Roger Pierrot).

tions. It is drawn from contemporary documents of all sorts: records of Balzac's dealings with publishers, personal and business accounts,[1] sketches by Balzac's relatives, acquaintances, friends and enemies; diaries, memoirs, other correspondences, critical articles—gossip, calumny and legend; and of course the store of still largely unedited material in the Collection Lovenjoul at Chantilly. Although no claim is made here to bring new facts or new documents to light, or to propose new interpretations of well-established ones, this volume is not modelled on any existing biography. At the same time I gladly acknowledge my deep indebtedness to that most enthusiastic and learned of English Balzacians, Mr. H. O. Stutchbury, for placing at my disposal his copious biographical note-books, compiled over a long period of time with constant attentiveness to all relevant publications. He may in fact claim a truly paternal interest in this volume, for he has immensely facilitated my access to that confusing mass of information, whether attested or apocryphal, from which a biographer of Balzac, however modest the scope of his work, must quarry. He has thus lightened the task of drawing a more or less concise and coherent story from a life which is well-nigh unmanageable in the variety of its minutiae. I thank him not only for this, but also for the generous interest he has taken in the composition of the book, for the observations and criticisms which his encyclopaedic knowledge of the subject has made extremely pertinent.

I am grateful also to another valued friend and counsellor, that eminent Balzacian scholar, the Abbé Philippe Bertault, for benevolent sympathy and helpful discussion of possibili-

[1] Notably R. Bouvier and Ed. Maynial, *Les Comptes dramatiques de Balzac*, 1938. Lovenjoul's *Histoire des Œuvres de H. de B.*, indispensable for the study of the Works, is also useful for many points of the Life.

ties; and to M. Jean Pommier for his kindness and courtesy in facilitating my access to documents in the Bibliothèque Lovenjoul at Chantilly. Nor do I forget the generosity of the Council of the Royal Holloway College in granting me a year of freedom; nor the encouragement given by my wife during moments of diffidence or despondency; nor the unflagging zeal of Miss Mary Pemberton in bringing the typescript to its ultimate state of legibility; nor the invaluable help given by the officers of the Athlone Press in the preparation and publication of the volume.

Royal Holloway College   H. J. H.
  University of London
        June 1956

CONTENTS

Contents

ABBREVIATIONS

It has not been considered necessary to refer to sources for the well-authenticated facts and incidents of Balzac's life, but some works frequently cited in the footnotes are abbreviated as follows:

Conard   *Œuvres complètes de Honoré de Balzac* (M. Bouteron and H. Longnon, 40 vols. 8°, Conard, 1912–40).

Conard O.D.   The three volumes of *Œuvres diverses* in the above edition.

Ed. Déf.   *Œuvres complètes de H. de B.*, 24 vols. 8°, Calmann Lévy, 1869–76: the erstwhile 'Edition définitive'. Only t. XXII (Prefaces, etc.) is utilized here.

E.   *Lettres à l'Étrangère* (M. Bouteron, 4 vols. 1899–1947, Calmann Lévy).

H.O.   Spoelberch de Lovenjoul, *Histoire des Œuvres* (2nd edition, 1886).

L.F.   *Lettres à sa famille*, 1809–50 (W. S. Hastings, 1950 edition, Albin Michel).

Z.C.   *Honoré de Balzac. Correspondance avec Zulma Carraud* (M. Bouteron, 1951 edition, Gallimard).

The place of publication is only given for works published elsewhere than at Paris.

I

FORMATIVE YEARS, 1799–1829

> *. . . génie ou sans génie, je me prépare des*
> *chagrins. Sans génie, je suis flambé. Il faudra*
> *toute ma vie sentir les désirs, n'être qu'un*
> *homme médiocre, me rejeter sur la fortune,*
> *que de soins! que de peines! Si j'ai du génie, je*
> *me vois d'avance, errant, persécuté, sans*
> *asyle, martyr de Dame Vérité, mais made-*
> *moiselle la Gloire me récompensera.*
>
> Lettres à sa famille, 25 Nov. 1819

i. Tours: Vendôme: Paris. 1799–1820

HONORÉ BALZAC was born on the 20th of May 1799 in
Tours. His family, originally Balssa, had its roots, not in
Touraine, but in Languedoc, in the region of Albi;[1] it was
of unmixed peasant stock. Although Honoré's father, Bernard-François, staked momentary claims, and Honoré himself a permanent one from 1830, to the supposedly aristocratic particle *de*, the family had no traceable connections,
either with that of the seventeenth-century moralist, Jean-
Louis Guez de Balzac, or with the Balzacs of Entragues
whose armorial bearings Honoré sought to annex.[2]

Bernard-François Balssa, who later normalized his patro-
nymic to Balzac, had come up to Paris in 1767 as an
attorney's clerk to make a career. He made it, before the
Revolution of 1789, as a functionary in that immense pre-

[1] It was at Albi in August 1819 that an uncle of Honoré, Louis Balssa,
was guillotined for the murder of a drab. This much-quoted fact has no
visible relevance either to Balzac's life or his work.

[2] For a somewhat blustering defence by Honoré of his aristocratic
claims see in the *Ed. Déf.* t. XXII, 441–3, his *Historique du Procès du
'Lys dans la Vallée'*, 16 June 1836. See also Louis de Grandmaison, in
Le Figaro, 6 June 1924, 'La particule de H. de B.'

Revolutionary administrative machine known as the *Conseil du Roi*. By 1788 he was 'greffier' and 'secrétaire' in that Council, and in 1791 was secretary to the Naval Minister, Bertrand de Molleville.[1] The vicissitudes and dangers of the later Revolutionary years diverted him to activities concerned with military supplies. The forbears of his wife, Anne-Charlotte-Laure Sallambier, whom he married in 1797, were cloth-merchants, but the family had promoted itself to that vast and indeterminate class of civil servants whose number Revolution and Empire only served to swell. Just before Honoré's birth, the Balzac couple migrated to Tours, where Bernard-François held various fiscal and administrative appointments; but in 1814 he returned to Paris to take up a post in the military commissariat under the aegis of his old friend and benefactor, the banker and army-contractor, Doumerc, the father of a woman (Mme Delannoy) who in later years was to be very generous to Honoré. The speculations that Bernard-François made on Doumerc's advice made a hole in his financial resources. When he retired in 1819 he and his family moved to Villeparisis, a small town outside Paris on the way to Meaux. There they remained three years, went back to Paris in the autumn of 1822, returned once more to Villeparisis in the spring of 1824, and moved in the summer of 1826 to Versailles to be near their elder daughter Laure, since 1820 the wife of an engineer, Eugène Surville. Laure was a year younger than Honoré. From infancy he was passionately attached to her, corresponded regularly with her in his adolescent years and visited her at Bayeux when she and her husband were living there. A second daughter, Laurence, whom Honoré nick-named 'Milady Plum-Pudding', made an unhappy marriage in 1821 and died in 1825. The remaining child of the Bal-

---

[1] *Les Études balzaciennes*, Sept.–Dec. 1951, *Calendrier*, p. 42.

zacs was Honoré's younger brother, Henri, probably fathered not by Bernard-François, but by a M. de Margonne, who used to visit them at Tours, and who owned a manor in Touraine, the Château de Saché, where, in later years, Honoré was often a guest. Henri, a spoilt child, was destined to be the ne'er-do-well of the family.

The Balzacs lived in fairly easy circumstances, at any rate until Bernard-François' retirement. The latter was an eccentric person, a 'philosophe', Voltairian in outlook, and a freemason; moderately tolerant as regards religion, the author of various quaint pamphlets.[1] His chief aims in life were to reach his century, which he missed by seventeen years, and to reap the full benefit of the investment he had made in the famous 'tontine Lafarge'—a tontine was one of the earlier forms of life-insurance. Honoré inherited from his father a remarkable energy of body and liveliness of mind. His robustness of temperament, coarseness of fibre, multiplicity of interests—sociological, physiological, biological—his opinionativeness, and a predisposition to wild ideas and manias, were intensified by contact with his father in his formative years. Honoré's relations with his mother, thirty-two years younger than her husband, were less happy. In accordance with the prevalent custom, she sent her son (and then Laure) to a wet-nurse, with whom they remained until Honoré was four. She was in some respects a conscientious parent, and by looking after his interests, when he required it, after he became a man, she made up for the stringency with which she appears to have treated him during childhood. But she was a nervous, unstable, irritable and hypochondriacal creature; somewhat mercenary, and

[1] *Mémoire sur le scandaleux désordre causé par les jeunes filles trompées et abandonnées* . . . (c. 1808); *Histoire de la Rage et moyen d'en préserver, comme autrefois, les hommes* (1809, reprinted by Honoré in 1826), etc.

3

from the first moment incapable of understanding and guiding the genius to whom she had given birth. The remark of Honoré's first mistress, Laure de Berny (if indeed she made it)[1]—'vous êtes une fleur venue sur du fumier . . . vous êtes un oeuf d'aigle couvé chez des oies' puts a natural comment rather too crudely. Honoré seems to have owed largely to his mother an early acquaintance with the pseudo-mystic fads of the age—mesmerism, magnetism, somnambulism, illuminism and various other forms of occultism—thanks to treatises with which her bookshelves were well stocked. But the chief impression we get of her relations with her son is one of frequent reprimands, reproaches and exasperating advice. Apart therefore from the remarkable sympathy and understanding which existed between Honoré and his sister Laure, he seems to have been brought up in a not too congenial family atmosphere. Many of his love affairs, with women of mature and usually maternal standing, seem to have been prompted by an urge, conscious or otherwise, to replace in his life the motherly love and care which he missed in infancy. In *La Femme de trente ans*, *Le Lys dans la vallée* and elsewhere the adult writer emphasizes the contrast between 'la maternité du devoir' and 'la maternité du cœur'; the implication in many of his letters is that he was deprived of the latter. They were written in moods of self-pity, and no doubt the complaint was exaggerated.

There is, indeed, some ground for supposing that Honoré was an intractable child. At the age of eight (22 June 1807) he was sent to the Oratorian College at Vendôme, where he spent nearly six years. He has given, in *Louis Lambert*, a half-jovial, half-pathetic, partly-romanticized account of his life there. With its quasi-conventual discipline it was

[1] We have only Balzac's word for it: *E.*, ii, 311; iii, 177.

naturally crude and coarse from the physical point of view. Honoré was indisciplined and resistant as a scholar, and unco-operative as a playmate. He spent much of his time in the College detention-rooms, which gave him ample opportunity for voracious and unguided reading. It is a disputed question whether a precocious interest in philosophy, psycho-physiology and mysticism inspired him, as it inspired Louis Lambert, his 'other self', to attempt a *Traité de la volonté*. In any case an excess of reading provoked a crisis in his health which necessitated his recall to Tours in April 1813. He had not been home once in all these years, and according to his own testimony his mother visited him only twice at school. As Vendôme is only thirty-five miles from Tours, this, if true, is a sad proof of maternal neglect.

He spent a year as a day-boy in the Lycée at Tours. The monarchy was restored in the spring of 1814, and as Bernard-François published a timely brochure in favour of the returning dynasty he got his job at Paris. The family took up their abode in the gloomy and sordid Marais quarter[1] (40 Rue du Temple) and Honoré was a boarder successively at two Paris 'internats' (the Pension Lepître and the Institut Sganzer et Beuzelin) as a result of which he obtained the contemporary equivalent of the modern 'baccalauréat-ès-lettres'. He then passed on, in November 1816, to studies at the Sorbonne with law as his speciality, although it appears, from Laure's biographical sketch and from *Louis Lambert*, that he also followed, with much interest, Victor Cousin's courses in philosophy. It was normal that he should be articled to a solicitor at the same time, and so he spent three years (1816–19) as a lawyer's clerk, first in the office

---

[1] Situated roughly east and north-east of the Halles. Formerly the abode of aristocrats and high-class courtesans, it was now mainly inhabited by the shop-keeping class. It became one of Balzac's most frequently described districts.

of Maître Guyonnet-Merville, to be immortalized in *Gobseck* and other stories as the prototype of the astute and upright lawyer, Derville; then (from April 1818) in that of a notary named Passez. Apprenticeship to a lawyer was the fate of many sons of the bourgeois. The prolific playwright, Eugène Scribe, had served his term with Guyonnet-Merville; and Jules Janin, later novelist, journalist and malevolent critic of Balzac himself, was there at the same time. Honoré took his duties lightly enough, but he had a serious illness in 1817, of which he was cured by Dr. Nacquart, throughout his life a loyal friend as well as his doctor. These three years must have been invaluable to this keen-eyed youth. While he joined in the pranks and minor dissipations of his fellow-clerks—such horse-play, practical jokes and escapades as are described in *Le colonel Chabert* and *Un Début dans la vie*—he was able not only to rub shoulders with all the varied followers of the law, but also to study the diverse types of humanity that pass through a lawyer's hands. He also acquired such a knowledge of the 'Code Civil' and legal procedure as was to give a characteristic structure and flavour to many of his novels.

But Honoré refused to settle down in the legal profession. Not for him the slow ascent to wealth and power which he described later in *La Physiologie du mariage*.

Le notaire du village . . . envoie son fils faire son droit à Paris; le bonnetier veut que son fils soit notaire; l'avocat destine le sien à la magistrature; le magistrat veut être ministre pour doter ses enfants de la pairie.

The urge to write was so strong in him that he prevailed upon his father to sanction a two-years' experiment. While they were at Villeparisis, he was to win his spurs as an incipient author, living on the very margin of subsistence (1,500 francs per annum), in an attic at 9 Rue Lesdiguières, a stone's throw west of the Place de la Bastille. He installed himself there after a preliminary sojourn at Nogent in the Isle-Adam, at the home of a family friend, the genial ex-abbé de Villers-la-Faye.

While occupied with his legal studies, he had been scribbling notes on philosophy and religion. He was soon trying his hand at shapeless and turgid fragments of novels in which 'philosophy' of the Encyclopaedist brand kept uneasy company with occultist fantasy. But he elected to prove his capacity as an emulator of Racine, though the subject he chose for a five-act tragedy, *Cromwell*, was more in the vein of Corneille, especially since this tragedy was to be 'le bréviaire des rois et des peuples.' His letters to Laure during this period are a precious source of information about his activities, hopes, projects and changing moods. It is at once amusing and touching to see 'Sophocle cadet', with 'la Nouvelle Héloïse pour maîtresse, La Fontaine pour ami, Boileau pour Juge, et le Père Lachaise pour me promener', straining to achieve the sublime and the pathetic; eking out his pennies, sweltering in summer, freezing in winter, with the future archaeologist Jules de Pétigny, and his elderly friend Théodore Dablin, former hardware-merchant and amateur art-collector (Pillerault in *César Birotteau*) to visit him occasionally and advise him. Alexandrines came reluctantly to Balzac as they did to Stendhal, and his efforts at drama were nearly all doomed to failure. In May 1820 he submitted *Cromwell* to the family judgment, and, when that was unfavourable, to the professional verdict of Andrieux of the Collège de France, who advised Mme Balzac to dissuade her son from writing. Honoré was undismayed. 'Les tragédies ne sont pas mon fort, voilà tout', he said, and decided to take to the novel. His parents were still indulgent, but they recalled him from the Rue Lesdiguières in December 1820, and then deprived him of his garret. For some time to come he lived almost wholly with his people.

His seventeen months of seclusion in a garret, with occasional sojourns at Villeparisis or L'Isle-Adam, enabled him to run about Paris, browse on the Quays or in libraries, and, on rare occasions, when he could scrape together the price of a ticket, to visit a theatre. They helped him to develop his extraordinary powers of observation—the story *Facino Cane* (1836) records the intuitive detective-work he did on casual passers-by. They brought out in him not only the student of living persons, but also the archaeologist of the 'Comédie Humaine', eminently capable of preserving the memory of forgotten corners of the ancient and changing metropolis. They also taught him what poverty meant, for himself, his neighbours, the down-at-heel and the half-starved.

Lorsque, entre onze heures et minuit, je rencontrais un ouvrier et sa femme revenant ensemble de l'Ambigu-Comique, je m'amusais à les suivre. . . . Ces braves gens parlaient d'abord de la pièce qu'ils avaient vue; de fil en aiguille, ils arrivaient à leurs affaires; la mère tirait son enfant par la main, sans écouter ni ses plaintes ni ses demandes; les deux époux comptaient l'argent qui leur serait payé le lendemain, ils le dépensaient de vingt manières différentes. C'était alors des détails de ménage, des doléances sur le prix excessif des pommes de terre, ou sur la longueur de l'hiver et le renchérissement des mottes, des représentations énergiques sur ce qui était dû au boulanger; enfin des discussions qui s'envenimaient, et où chacun d'eux déployait son caractère en mots pittoresques. En entendant ces gens, je pouvais épouser leur vie, je me sentais leurs guenilles sur le dos, je marchais les pieds dans leurs souliers percés; leurs désirs, leurs besoins, tout passait dans mon âme, ou mon âme passait dans la leur. C'était le rêve d'un homme éveillé. Je m'échauffais avec eux contre les chefs d'atelier qui les tyrannisaient, ou contre les mauvaises pratiques qui les faisaient revenir plusieurs fois sans les payer. Quitter ses habitudes, devinir un autre que soi par l'ivresse des facultés morales, et jouer ce jeu à volonté, telle était ma distraction.[1]

The second phase of his literary apprenticeship began when he was introduced, late in 1820 or early in 1821, to a type of literary adventurer already beginning to swarm in the French capital, Auguste Le Poitevin de l'Égreville, or Le Poitevin Saint-Alme. From this man Honoré got the hope of turning literature into a money-making concern, by adopting a method of literary collaboration and catering for cruder tastes. It seems probable that his prospect of really paying his way as 'écrivain public et poète français, à deux francs la page', induced his parents to indulge his whim instead of flinging him back into a lawyer's office or injecting him into the civil service.

For three or four years Honoré knocked together a large but indefinite number of fourth-rate novels in collaboration with Le Poitevin, Étienne Arago and other scribbler-journalists. Even Laure Surville and her husband took an occasional hand. One cannot but regret that Balzac was deterred from continuing as he had begun and hammering out a technique and style with more scrupulous artistic zeal. For this the incomprehension of his parents and his own impatience for wealth are to blame.

J'ai l'espoir de devenir riche à coups de romans. Quelle chute! Pourquoi faut-il que je n'aye pas 1,500 livres de rente, pour pouvoir travailler d'une manière glorieuse! Enfin, il faut s'indépendantiser, et je n'ai que cet ignoble moyen-là: salir du papier et faire gémir la presse.[2]

Sometimes indeed he thought of a political career, or sighed for a rich marriage as a short-cut to fortune. Yet his work as a literary hack served its turn. Perhaps Balzac, unlike his contemporary Victor Hugo, 'enfant sublime', must by nature have been slow in bringing to fruition the genius

---

[1] *Facino Cane*, Conard xvi, 372–3.   [2] *L. F.* 52, Aug. 1821.

latent within him, of which he seems to have been conscious even in childhood. The series of novels signed by 'Auguste de Viellerglé' (anagram of l'Égreville), 'Viellerglé et Lord R'Hoone', 'Lord R'Hoone', 'Viellerglé de Saint-Alme', etc., helped Balzac to acquire the rudiments of his future craft. When writing on his own account he used the pen-names of 'Lord R'Hoone' (anagram of Honoré) and 'Horace de Saint-Aubin'. His literary models were, from the first, Sir Walter Scott (notably *Ivanhoe* and *Kenilworth*), sentimental novelists like Maria Edgeworth (*Belinda*), and also the creators of the novel of terror, especially Anne Radcliffe, 'Monk' Lewis and Maturin, author of *Melmoth the Wanderer*, a work of diabolical propensities which made a lasting impression on Balzac. For a life-long Anglophobe, he was extraordinarily addicted to English authors, whom he could read only in translation. As for French writers, his immediate models were other blood-curdling novelists like Ducray-Duminil, and exploiters of the 'roman gai', like Pigault-Lebrun and the coming best-seller, Paul de Kock.

Inspiration came also from writers of greater stature than these latter: from Rabelais and Sterne for the boisterous or insinuating humour which sometimes informed his tone and style; from Rousseau, who taught him to glorify passion, and at times to declaim against the artificialities and corruptness of civilized society; from the Richardson of *Clarissa*, from the Byron of *Lara* and *Manfred*, the Goethe of *Werther* and *Faust*; and probably, even at this early stage, from Diderot and the less reputable Laclos, and possibly also the still less reputable Marquis de Sade. This is only a selective list. The influence of Hoffmann, the writer of fantastic tales, and the American Fenimore Cooper, author of *The Last of the Mohicans*, was to assert itself in due course. He was to yield far more to the fascination of

Rabelais, while Molière and Beaumarchais must also be counted among his gods. Balzacian experts, MM. L.-J. Arrigon, P. Barrière, A. Prioult and M. Bardèche, have minutely examined such of these pseudo-historical, sensational or parodistic novels as are obviously or probably the products of Balzac's pen, and have patiently elaborated a picture of Balzac learning painfully and gradually the tricks of structure, composition, dialogue, character-portrayal and background-description which led up to the seemingly miraculous blossoming of 1829.[1] Perhaps in this process a note of wistfulness is perceptible here and there, especially in prefaces and notes, revealing a mixture of diffidence and self-assertiveness; a ruefulness arising from a sense of his present obscurity, contrasted with his evident ambition for fame and gain.

ii. Hack writer: publisher: printer. 1820–8

It is thus arguable that such 'cochonneries littéraires' (Balzac's own term) of 1821 as *Les deux Hector ou Les deux Familles bretonnes*, *Charles Pointel ou Mon Cousin de la main gauche*, *L'Héritière de Birague*, *Jean-Louis ou La Fille trouvée*, and many others in which Balzac had at least a hand, were by no means a waste of time and energy. What then of the independent works which he could claim as his own? *Sténie, ou les Erreurs philosophiques* (probably 1820–1; unfinished and unpublished until 1936)[2] is *La nouvelle Héloïse* melodramatized, with a Saint-Preux who is also a Werther and a Byronic rebel, a Julie from whom has been ripped out the stuffing that, after her first fault, made her so formidably resistant to Saint-Preux, and a Wolmar-

---

[1] *Les Débuts littéraires de H. de B.* (1924); *H. de B. Les romans de jeunesse* (1928); *B. avant la Comédie Humaine* (1936); *B. romancier* (1940; reprinted 1950).
[2] Edited by M. A. Prioult (Courville).

Bomston (two philosophic males rolled into the person of De Vanehr) who has become the apostle of atheism, materialism and individualism. The *Falthurne* manuscripts (1820; 1823–4; not published till 1950)[1] are two distinct fragments which offer only disparate blends of philosophy, science, illuminism and fiction. *Le Centenaire ou Les deux Béringheld* (1822) is, in intention, a thriller, but in the background lurks, as in *Falthurne*, the theory of magnetism, 'fluide vital', etc. which was to become part of Balzac's stock-in-trade. *Clotilde de Lusignan ou Le beau Juif* (1822) is a servile imitation of *Ivanhoe*, without Scott's good qualities. *La dernière Fée ou La nouvelle Lampe merveilleuse* (1823), which paints a gullible innocent bewitched by a sophisticated English duchess, gives us some idea of the distance Balzac has to travel before he can write a story like *Les Secrets de la Princesse de Cadignan*. *Wann-Chlore* (finished 1824, published 1825) is a romantically impossible story leading up to a situation which Balzac dwells on with relish—that of a man with two wives, both of whom love him to distraction. *Le Vicaire des Ardennes* (1822) with its sequel *Annette et le criminel* (1824), begins as a blend of sentimental novel and satire on manners, then develops into a full-blooded 'roman noir' as the implacable murderer, Argow the Pirate (a compound of Byron's *Corsair*, Scott's *Pirate* and Godwin's *Caleb Williams*) gets into stride and progresses from malevolent jealousy, through redeeming love and religious conversion, to death on the scaffold. These works[2] are not good novels, and yet they are not uninteresting or unprofitable to read. They show a young mind in a curious state of ebullience; a wild imagination ignoring or dispensing with

[1] By P. G. Castex (José Corti).

[2] When in 1836 Souverain published the works of 'Horace de Saint-Aubin', *Le Centenaire* became *Le Sorcier*; *Wann-Chlore* became *Jane la pâle*; *Annette et le criminel* became *Argow le pirate*.

verisimilitude of action and character, pandering to a juvenile taste for rhetorical effusiveness and thinly-disguised eroticism; hovering perilously but ecstatically over the theme of incestuous passion; sometimes carrying denunciation of the social pact and declaration of lovers' rights to a point that would have shocked Rousseau; atheist, occultist, libertine, sentimentalist, anti-clerical, fulsomely pious and edifying by turns. And yet he frequently shows signs of a capacity to conceive real people, and a knack of hitting off human habits and foibles. *Le Vicaire des Ardennes* is, in its beginning, a 'scene of country life', and in a crude way he often anticipates some of the most successful themes of the 'Comédie Humaine', in particular *La Femme abandonnée* (*Wann-Chlore*), and *Mémoires de deux jeunes mariées* (*La dernière Fée*). That *Le Vicaire des Ardennes* and *Annette et le criminel* should point forward to 'le Capitaine parisien' in *La Femme de trente ans* and to certain aspects of *Splendeurs et misères des courtisanes* does not redound so clearly to the credit of the more mature Balzac.

A fresh orientation in Balzac's interests becomes visible about 1824, the year when, through the final withdrawal of his parents from Paris, he achieved physical but not financial independence from his family and took rooms in the Rue de Tournon. Two strangely conservative-minded pamphlets that he produced this year (*Du Droit d'aînesse*, in February; *Histoire impartiale des Jésuites*, in April) may be explained, partly as tasks undertaken for payment, and partly by the influence of a Catholic and royalist friend, Jean Thomassy. But it is surprising to see him at this early moment professing views on 'Throne and Altar' which he was not to adopt firmly until eight years later. He was even, at this time, working on a *Traité de la prière*, a strange exercise for a young determinist who had so recently argued Providence out of court, and whose knowledge of his subject-matter was so manifestly second-hand. Thomassy reproved him for making the attempt.[1] From 1824, however, it is Horace-Napoléon Raisson, another literary jobber, who comes into prominence and replaces Le Poitevin de l'Égreville as Balzac's collaborator and exploiter. Raisson's rôle was to divert him from the 'roman noir' and the 'roman gai', and to draw him in the direction of humorous, mock-didactic literature whose dominant note is the satire of social types and social conduct. That Balzac was of his own accord that way inclined is clear from certain parts of *Jean-Louis* and *Le Vicaire des Ardennes*. Already a work, as yet without title, an early version of *La Physiologie du mariage*, begun about 1824, and printed by Balzac himself in 1826 or 1827 (it is known today as the 'édition préoriginale') exploits this vein to the full.

As a sequel to the work of the Encyclopaedists and their successors, the 'ideologists' of Imperial times, and thanks to the publication of anatomical and medical treatises by doctors like Bichat and Broussais, a considerable amount of theorizing went on, during the early years of the nineteenth century, about the relation between brain-structure and thought and, more generally, between mind and matter. The ideologist Georges Cabanis had already laid the foundations of this new subject of investigation: psycho-physiology. A Swiss thinker, Jean-Gaspard Lavater, had invented a new 'science'—'physiognomy'—whose basic principle was that a person's character, and indeed his destiny, are to be read in his physical features. A German doctor, Francis-Joseph Gall, added to this the supposed science of 'phrenology', which

---

[1] None the less, the Abbé Philippe Bertault, in the Introduction to his critical edition of this unpublished fragment (Boivin, 1942) shows how clearly the *Traité de la prière* points forward to the 'mystic books' of 1831–5, *Louis Lambert* and *Séraphita*.

attempted to map out the human brain and deduce character and temperament from the conformation of the skull.
Thanks to these men, there was coming into vogue a practice of writing devoted to the description of human manners,
habits and eccentricities, usually in a humorous vein. Its
pseudo-scientific pretensions were revealed in the titles
adopted; 'physiologies', 'anatomies', 'pathologies'. It was no
doubt Brillat-Savarin's world-famous treatise on gastro-
nomy, *La Physiologie du goût* (1825), that suggested the
title, though not the substance, of the work just mentioned,
Balzac's *La Physiologie du mariage*. The publication of
the latter in 1829 was to give further encouragement to the
vogue of 'physiologies'. Even more popular, however, was
the analogy offered to frivolous writers by the forms and
formulas of jurisprudence. The 'Code Civil', that vast syste-
matisation of the laws of France carried out under the Convention Nationale and Napoleon, had now been in operation
for some years, and the fashion arose of parodying the Code
in satirical manuals professing to give guidance to individuals
in their relations with the society of the day. It is here that
Raisson comes in most conspicuously, for between 1825 and
1830, probably using Balzac as a literary ghost in most cases,
he flooded the market with 'Codes', or with analogous hand-
books known as 'Arts'. Among them may be noted *Le Code
civil, Manuel complet de la politesse* (1825) *Le Code galant,
ou l'Art de conter fleurette* (1829), *Le Code conjugal* (1829),
Le Code des commis-voyageurs (1830). The earliest of such
Codes—*Le Code des gens honnêtes, ou l'Art de ne pas être
dupe des fripons*, published anonymously in March 1825, is
undoubtedly pure Balzac.[1] So, probably, are such 'Arts' as
L'Art de mettre sa cravate (1827), and *L'Art de payer ses*

---

[1] Raisson's name appeared in an edition of 1829, but in 1854 it was
republished as belonging to Balzac.

dettes (1827).[1] Briefly, the idea of the *Code des gens honnêtes* was to assemble, and to punctuate with cynical aphorisms and 'axioms', accounts of the many ways of fleecing one's neighbours, ranging from pocket-picking and confidence-tricks to the peculations, extortions and swindles of doctors, priests, lawyers, small-scale and large-scale financiers. The thesis so much harped-upon in this work, namely, that the most successful breakers of the Eighth Commandment are those who keep on the windy side of the law, was to become one of the most recurrent points in Balzac's denunciation of human society.

For a short time Balzac contributed in 1826 to *Le Figaro*, an impudent and politically-tendentious journal recently founded by Étienne Arago and Maurice Alhoy, and destined to an exciting and chequered career for the next seven years. He also, according to M. Prioult, had a hand in, if he did not wholly compose, various historical novels appearing in 1827 and 1828 under the names of Horace Raisson and others. Certain it is that the future historian of his own times cherished, and often returned to, the idea of writing a whole cycle of novels which should resuscitate aspects of the fif-teenth, sixteenth and seventeenth centuries.[2] Nor had he quite abandoned the hope of making his name as a play-wright, for in 1822 and 1824 he had written the unacted melodramas *Le Nègre* and *Le Lazaroni*. But between 1825 and 1828 he became involved in a disastrous experiment. At the instigation of a well-to-do friend of the family, d'Assonvillez de Rougemont, and not without encourage-

[1] Balzac was to learn more about this 'art' as time went on. See Baude-laire's sketch of 1846: *Comment on paie ses dettes quand on a du génie.* (ed. *Pléiade*, ii, 390 ff).
[2] One of these, *L'Excommunié*, dealing with the Armagnac-Bur-gundian civil strife of the fifteenth century, was partly written up by Balzac and completed for the Souverain edition of 1836 by one of Balzac's amanuenses, the Marquis de Belloy.

ment from his parents, he tried to make his fortune as a businessman. First of all as a publisher: he joined an association with Urbain Canel (who had published *Wann-Chlore*) and others for the production of one-volume editions of the great classics—La Fontaine and Molière. But the time was not yet ripe for omnibus-editions, especially when the pages were in tiny print and double columns, and poorly illustrated—although the illustrations were drawn by a young man of rising talent, Achille Devéria. The venture quickly failed.

In 1826 Balzac bought a printing-press, with André Barbier, a foreman-printer, as a partner to run the technical side, and set up his abode on the premises, in the present Rue Visconti, north of Saint-Germain des Prés. The list of books he printed, apart from ordinary jobbing-work and prospectuses for patent medicines, is varied and interesting. It includes renderings from the German by Loève-Weimars, the future translator of Hoffmann, a translation of some of Maturin's lesser novels, Mérimée's *La Jacquerie*, and the third edition of Vigny's *Cinq-Mars*. He thus came into initial though, it seems, not very cordial contact with these two writers whose reputation was already established. In September 1827 he bought a bankrupt type-foundry behind Saint-Sulpice, in the Rue Garancière.

Anyone else might have made a success of these ventures, which were sound enough in themselves. But Balzac had to borrow money from many quarters, including his family, to finance them, and in those days an insufficiency of specie and paper currency, which had to be supplemented by paper credit of all sorts, resulted in complications which only too easily led to the bankruptcy court. Balzac himself kept the books of these concerns, and he was just the wrong man to do it. He was too accommodating with customers, too ready to sink new credit in brilliant ancillary schemes or inventions, and he was incapable of keeping his own private accounts separate from those of the firm—his personal expenditure was beginning to soar on the strength of his hopes. The result was that his partners looked upon him as an unreliable associate, and backed out as soon as prospects became gloomy. Canel, himself on the verge of temporary failure, left him in 1826 with a debt of some 9,000 francs and a lot of unsold classics on his hands. Balzac incautiously disposed of some of them to a bookseller who paid him in bills drawn by two other booksellers, well knowing that they were insolvent. Barbier in his turn withdrew from the printing partnership on terms which enabled him to buy up the concern for himself a few months later. By April 1828 it was clear that Balzac's business-career must come to an end.

He emerged with a very large liability, bordering on a hundred thousand francs, about £4,000, a sum which for its purchasing power was then worth nearly four times what it is in 1956,[1] a lot of it being owed to his mother. This became the foundation of his life-long indebtedness. A normal man might have paid it off in a few years, but it was swollen year by year from 1831 onwards by Balzac's incorrigible and ever-mounting extravagance. He was destined to be the slave of money to the end of his days. But perhaps the experience these affairs gave him of trade and finance outweighs this disadvantage. He learnt to be wary of publisher-booksellers who extricated themselves from one bad venture by engaging in new ones and fobbed off their bad debts on commercial greenhorns; he took his revenge on them in *Un grand homme de province à Paris*.[2] He learnt what it meant to go round

[1] The franc of this period may be multiplied by about 200 or more to obtain a rough idea of its general purchasing power in terms of the franc of 1956.

[2] *Illusions perdues*, pt. II (1839).

hat in hand begging for credit, to be threatened with legal proceedings by his own workmen for arrears of wages, and to have the disgrace of bankruptcy staring him in the face. He discovered something about the legal intricacies in which a man may become involved when he has both to meet his own obligations and recover debts from others. He acquired some first-hand knowledge of the procedure of liquidation. These experiences he amply exploited in many later works. His worries and woes as a printer find an echo in *L'Interdiction* (1836), and form the substance of *Les Souffrances de l'inventeur*.[1] The tragi-comic history of the imprudent businessman fleeced and forced into bankruptcy by sharks and crooks took shape eventually in *César Birotteau* (1837).

iii. Friendships and first loves

It is appropriate here to glance at Balzac's early sentimental life. Passages in *La Peau de chagrin* and *Le Lys dans la vallée* which are partly autobiographical suggest that he was not exempt from the usual troubles and temptations of puberty, and that his adolescence did not pass without one or two 'piquantes aventures', to use Laure Surville's expression. Yet, in spite of his tremendous physical vitality, he does not seem to have been sexually precocious, even though he sometimes claims to be as avid for love as he is for glory.[2] His letters to Laure in the 1820's are usually those of a young man full of energy and purpose, bursting with humour and animal spirits, already building castles in the air on the foundation of his literary efforts, with one ear cocked for the chance of an advantageous marriage. This correspondence also proves a deep and affectionate understanding between brother and sister which did not suffer eclipse until the last decade of his life.

[1] *Illusions perdues*, pt. III (1843). [2] *L. F.*, 53. Aug. 1821.

His friendship with a school friend of his sister's, Zulma Tourangin, wife of an artillery major, Carraud, director of studies at the Military School at Saint-Cyr, began about 1827 or 1828 at Versailles. While his parents and sister lived there he could pay frequent visits to Saint-Cyr and so lay the foundations of the truest and soundest friendship he was to enjoy. In 1831 Carraud was suspected of but lukewarm attachment to the new régime. He was relieved of his post at Saint-Cyr and put in charge of the government powder-factory near Angoulême—an exile which was to ensure some valuable country holidays for Balzac. Zulma was a rather angular-faced brunette, ugly by her own confession, though one can imagine the face and eyes (painted by Viénot in 1827) achieving charm and even beauty when animated by kindliness and affection. These she was to give in full measure to Balzac, as well as intelligent criticism, sound cautions and good advice. This was dictated by an unflinching honesty of character, and Honoré would often have done well to follow the counsels of so noble-hearted a woman. Her literary judgment was sensitive though not unimpeachable: her preference of *Louis Lambert* to Goethe's *Faust* was perhaps due to imperfect knowledge of the latter.[1]

Her pure and ardent friendship for Balzac, M. Bouteron has said, 'avait la puissance d'un amour', but in spite of a passing desire which Balzac had in the summer of 1832 to degrade the friendship, they were never lovers. Balzac's first and perhaps his sincerest love-affair began in June 1821, when he met Laure de Berny, née Hinner, daughter of a court harpist under Louis XVI and a tire-woman of Marie Antoinette.

As a child Laure Hinner lived close to the dangers of the Terror. Her mother and step-father, M. de Jarjayes, were

[1] *Z. C.,* 102–3.

involved in attempts to save the queen from the guillotine, and they all spent a short time in prison in 1794. She had been married in 1793 to Gabriel de Berny, and by 1821 had had ten children, one of whom was not her husband's. She was now forty-four years old and living at Villeparisis; and that is how Balzac came to know her. He was giving lessons to his brother Henri and her son Alexandre, and saw much of her. He quickly and passionately fell in love with this woman who was old enough to be his mother, who was in fact one year older than his mother. Always an advocate of the 'rights of nature', as he had already proclaimed in such works as *Le Vicaire des Ardennes*,[1] he laid violent siege to her affections with an odd mixture of passion and *gaucherie*. He was not very subtle in his love-making, as is shown by his hinting to her that a woman of forty-five who finds love knocking once more at the door of her heart has good cause for satisfaction. After some resistance, Laure de Berny opened that door in the summer of 1822, and it was to this woman—'La Dilecta', as he was to call her—that Balzac owed his real, as opposed to his bookish initiation into the sentimental and passionate life. Enough of their correspondence has survived[2] to prove that she gave herself over, body, heart and soul, to this unlicked cub with the magnetic eyes and the over-riding will.

The tie lasted until her death in 1836, although by 1832 it had ceased to have a physical basis, and the maternal element in it, evident from the first, alone subsisted. But, from 1822 to 1828 at least, she was his mistress, mentor, guide, friend, consoler, critic, and even his financial backer. She put capital into his business ventures of 1825 to 1827, visited, helped and com-

[1] '. . . l'on n'est jamais criminel en obéissant à la voix de la nature'—strange advice given by a curé to his assistant!

[2] It is given in Hanotaux and Vicaire, *La Jeunesse de Balzac*, edition of 1921.

forted him, deepened his romantic glorification of love into a sort of passionate mysticism, and brought to him some preliminary knowledge, not only of a woman's emotional potentialities, but also of the ways of the world and that upper-class society which was as yet a closed book to him. This statement is, however, subject to reservations. Mme de Berny did not convert him to royalism, nor could she admit him to aristocratic society. For their relations were unconventional even in the eyes of easy-going modernity; and she lived away from the world on uncomfortable terms with her difficult and uncongenial husband. But she understood Balzac and schooled him, and a sentence in one of her letters of 1828 is in itself a vivid characterization of the debt-ridden ex-printer:

Adieu, Didi, on t'aime quand même, on t'aime avec tes colères, avec tes miriades [*sic*] de caprices, avec tes manques d'usages, avec toutes les imperfections qu'on aime elles-mêmes, heureux d'avoir à te les pardonner pour que tu en pardonnes d'autres. On t'aime malgré la corde qui te manque, mais on t'adore pour toutes celles qui font vibrer ton gentil cœur et ta belle âme.

At that moment gratitude was the dominant note in the expression of Mme de Berny's affection. Jealousy also had its place, and was to do so almost to the end. In 1828 it was prompted by the growing importance in Honoré's life of the Duchesse d'Abrantès, widow of Napoleon's marshal, Junot. The young writer had met her about 1826. She was now forty-two and was hoping to mend her diminished fortunes by writing her *Mémoires*, rich in reminiscences, portraits and anecdotes of Imperial days. They began to appear in 1831, and Balzac himself wrote much of the first volume, found a publisher for it and took great pains in preparing other volumes for the press. Laure de Berny's resentment at this friendship did not prevent it from deepening into something more between 1828 and 1831, and Balzac acquired yet more material for his comprehension of women who had passed the prime of youthfulness and beauty. He was frequently to espouse their cause in the 'Comédie Humaine'. But the Duchess was to prove more useful than Mme de Berny herself in one respect, for she could procure him access to the drawing-rooms of important society hostesses. She could also furnish him with much private information about social life and political intrigue during the Directory and Empire, and afford him glimpses of what went on behind the scenes in the days of Napoleon. The anonymous author of *Balzac mis à nu*,[1] probably Lambinet, one-time mayor of Versailles, questions the value of the Duchess d'Abrantès' information, reducing it to 'fausses confidences, révélations déjà divulguées, anecdotes d'antichambres . . . jugements inexacts ou injustes'. But is not this the stuff of which novels are made? Whatever its quality, Balzac used it for such works as *L'Histoire des Treize*, *Une Conversation entre onze heures et minuit*, and above all, *Une ténébreuse Affaire*. Moreover the Duchess helped, in conjunction with the Carrauds and the journalist-novelist Hyacinthe de Latouche, first editor of André Chénier and soon to succeed Horace Raisson as Balzac's 'literary broker', to keep Balzac in sympathy with the Bonapartists.

[1] Published in 1928 with Preface and Notes by Charles Léger. This is one of those works which Balzac's biographers use freely, because the author writes as an eye-witness, and because he supplies a large amount of circumstantial detail about the persons with whom Balzac came into contact, especially at Versailles, from 1827 to 1841. But the whole work is extremely suspect. It was written after 1876, and the author's memory is often at fault over chronology. But this is the least of his defects. He is consistently hostile to Balzac as indeed to practically everyone of whom he writes, with the exception of Delphine de Girardin and Countess Guidoboni-Visconti. Scandal and spicy stories are meat and drink to him. The editor of the book (M. Léger) awards it unmerited credence. A curious feature is that Lambinet appears to have been unaware of Mme de Berny's existence.

iv. The dawn of success. 1828–9

In 1828 a cousin of the Balzacs, a notary named Sédillot, undertook to wind up Honoré's commercial affairs for him, and the type-foundry was ceded, in compensation for monies advanced and lost, to Alexandre de Berny, who made a successful business of it by dint of a few years' steady application, just as Barbier did with the printing-press. Balzac was free to give his whole mind to writing. In April of this year he began his seven years' tenancy of No. 1 Rue Cassini, near the Observatory, where he had a three-room flat on the second floor; for the time being, with Latouche's help, he decorated and furnished it on a modest scale, but as the years passed and his social pretensions grew, he turned it into a 'véritable bonbonnière'. He was still, as in 1825, meditating over the historical novel.

His mind was divided between two ventures. One of them, *Le Capitaine des Boutefeux*, was to resuscitate the anarchic period of the Hundred Years' War. The other, *Le Gars*, was to deal with the guerilla warfare between Revolution-aries and Royalists, 'Blues' and 'Whites', which had broken out in 1799 on the borders of Normandy and Brittany, in succession to the regular civil war which had raged in La Vendée during the years 1793–6. In 1827 Balzac had worked on *Le Gars*, and in the summer had written for it an *Aver-tissement*[1] under the name of Victor Morillot. This Intro-duction was semi-autobiographical in character, but gave a full explanation of what he thought the historical novel should be. France was on the threshold of a historically-minded age, and the new historians, such as Thierry, Guizot, Thiers, Michelet and Quinet, were unanimous in at least one respect: they revolted against the conception of history as a charnel-house in which were stored up the dry

[1] Published in 1931 by P. Abraham, in *Créatures chez Balzac*.

bones of historical facts. They went in for bold syntheses and audacious generalizations, attempting to draw from bare facts a dominant conception of the direction in which humanity had marched or was marching. In a word it was an age which abounded in 'philosophies of history'. Balzac too repudiated dry-as-dust history, and maintained that the business of a historical novelist was to unfold to a nation the meaning of its past, to show how the figures he used were representative of movements and ideas and thus, though of course he does not use the term, to present in his turn a 'philosophy of history'.

Latouche was at work on a novel of contemporary history, *Fragoletta, ou Naples en 1799*, which he published in 1829. He was good as a literary counsellor but mediocre as a literary creator. The criticism he gave Balzac was shortly after to be put at the service of a newcomer to the world of letters, George Sand. His influence as Balzac's mentor has been exaggerated,[1] but he undoubtedly was a greater figure in the world of letters than Le Poitevin or Raisson. He negotiated with Urbain Canel for the publication of the novel which Balzac, in September 1828, retired into the country to write. It was to centre round Fougères, and he obtained hospitality in that town from a General de Pommereul and his wife, who had ties of friendship and obligation with the Balzacs. He spent six weeks there getting local colour, surprised them by his personal shabbiness and eccentricity, delighted and entertained them with his lively good humour and the zest with which he improvised tales. The result was that *Le Gars* developed into *Le dernier Chouan ou La Bretagne en 1800*, published in March 1829: the first novel to appear under Balzac's real name. 'Le Gars' was the nickname by which the leader of the Royalist

---

[1] By F. Ségu, *Un Maître de Balzac méconnu: H. de Latouche*, 1928.

guerillas was known; 'Chouans' was the name given to the guerillas themselves because their favourite signal was the hooting of an owl. In 1834 Balzac carefully revised the work, and the second edition appeared under a different title: *Les Chouans, ou La Bretagne en 1799.* The 1829 version did not sell well, and as Latouche had risked money in the publication a quarrel arose which impaired the relations between him and Balzac; but the work was favourably reviewed in the press. *Le dernier Chouan* launched Balzac as an author in his own right.

Le dernier Chouan brought Balzac only a thousand francs, much of which went towards payment of debts. He lived for much of 1829 on the hospitality of friends. He became now a frequent visitor to the Margonnes at Saché. He later reported M. de Margonne to have been something of a miser, and his wife 'intolérante et dévote, bossue, peu spirituelle'. Margonne was no doubt conscious of a moral debt to the Balzac family, but he was fond of Honoré and was glad to give him opportunity for rest and recuperation, or for uninterrupted work, as the occasion demanded. It was from Saché that Balzac was recalled to Versailles to attend the funeral of his father, who died on June 19th 1829. On July 10th, according to Mme Victor Hugo's biography of her husband (written more or less at his dictation),[1] Balzac was present at their house in Paris for the reading to an assembly of literary and artistic stars—Sainte-Beuve, Vigny, Musset, Alexandre Dumas, Eugène Devéria, the lithographer Tony Johannot, etc.—of *Un Duel sous Richelieu* (the *Marion Delorme* of 1831), a play which was intended to carry the Romantic standard on to the Parisian theatre, but which was banned by the censorship and replaced by the hurriedly written *Hernani.* Then he left Paris again to stay with Mme

[1] *Victor Hugo raconté par un témoin de sa vie.*

de Berny at her country house, La Bouleaunière, near Nemours. He was again at Saché in September, and from there he went to meet the Duchesse d'Abrantès, with whom he was now on the most intimate terms, at Maffliers, where she was staying at the castle as a guest of the General Count Augustin de Talleyrand-Périgord. But during these visits he was applying himself to works which were to make him a fashionable author—the definitive *Physiologie du mariage* and his first *Scènes de la vie privée*. *La Physiologie du mariage* ('par un jeune célibataire'—this anonymity was soon penetrated) appeared in December 1829. It obtained a 'succès de scandale', and for a time shocked the serious-minded Zulma Carraud. The six 'Scènes' were published in two volumes by Mame and Delaunay in April 1830. The fact that they include the original versions of *Gobseck*, *La Vendetta* and *La Maison du chat qui pelote* indicates that Balzac was now standing on the threshold of his 'Comédie Humaine'.

II

DECISIVE YEARS, 1830–33

> *. . . Les artistes sont en général des meurt-de-*
> *faim. Ils sont trop dépensiers pour ne pas être*
> *toujours de mauvais sujets.*
>
> La Maison du chat qui pelote

i. The significance of 1830

VICTOR HUGO, in disdain of his own 'juvenilia', dated his birth as a poet from about his twentieth year. If we assign Balzac's 'birth' to the eve of 1830, we may say that he was entering the literary world at a truly exciting moment, revolutionary as regards literature, politics and social consciousness.

The 25th February 1830 is the date when the battle for a new literature reached its highest pitch, over the first performance of *Hernani*, with Classicists and Romantics hurling insults and missiles at one another's heads in the pit and galleries of the Théâtre-Français. Not that French Romanticism came into being in 1830. As a spiritual renaissance, as a restatement of intellectual, sentimental, moral and religious values it had been gathering momentum for seventy years. It had borrowed inspiration from home and abroad, from Jean-Jacques Rousseau and Bernardin de Saint-Pierre, from the melancholy nature-loving English poets, from the poets of 'Sturm und Drang' in Germany. It had turned again to England for the extravaganzas of Anne Radcliffe, Lewis, etc. It had drawn nourishment from the indigenous melodramas of the Revolutionary period, and from the terror and turbulence of the Revolution itself. In the early years of the

Restoration, Scott with his historical resuscitations, and Byron with his now passionate, now cynical defiance of accepted values, had come into the picture. The progress of Romanticism is marked by great names—Mme de Staël. Chateaubriand, Senancour and Benjamin Constant. It owes much to philosophers and seers such as De Bonald, Joseph de Maistre and Ballanche. It asserts the value of individual experience and the right of self-exploration in the domain of art. It stands for the glorification of sentiment and passion and the renewal of religious enthusiasm. It often pleads the cause of Catholicism, though its Catholicism is tinged with dangerous heresies and suspect forms of mysticism. Some of its adherents are recognizable by their incurable melancholy —the *mal du siècle*. Others are violently impatient with the present, yearn for an irrecoverable past or strain after an unimaginable future. Many of them adore Byron, and affect a Titanic, a Satanic rebelliousness. To most of these tendencies of thought and feeling Balzac, despite his basic fidelity to Encyclopaedic rationalism, had been intermittently responsive since he first began to write.

It was not until about 1824 that Romanticism became self-conscious as an aesthetic movement and launched its attack upon the modes, conventions and technique of Classicism, with Victor Hugo, inspired by Shakespeare, moving rapidly to the vanguard and uttering his war-cry 'Mettons le marteau dans les théories, les poétiques et les systèmes'. To support him in 1830 in his fight for a new drama rallied the group of youthful extravagants, wild, hirsute, gaudy, noisy and blatant, known as 'les Jeune-France'. Having Gérard de Nerval and Théophile Gautier as their fuglemen, and such eccentrics and eventual failures as Célestin Nanteuil, Bouchardy, Théophile Dondey and Petrus Borel as their stalwarts, they made it their business to mock at the Academicians, shock the bourgeois, rout the Philistines, and proclaim the sacred right of the 'artist' to live his life, pursue his art, and exploit his particular medium exactly as he pleased.

Apart from Nerval and Gautier, they were only the froth on the surface of a great movement, for their most notable achievement was by their pranks and pretensions to provide anecdotes for literary historians. Once the noise of battle rolled away they ceased to count. The year 1830 is marked as the threshold of an age when writers of genius come to the fore and begin to show their quality. Lamartine, Vigny and Hugo are already in the limelight. Musset makes his bow, or rather his pert grimace as a precocious Byron, before settling down to more independent poetry and drama. George Sand is waiting in the wings. Michelet and Quinet are about to turn history into a matter for passionate philosophy and speculation. The Catholic revivalist Lamennais is about to startle Christendom by his rapid advance towards the democratic mysticism of *Les Paroles d'un croyant*. So great is their exuberance, so full is the spate of their inspiration, so voluminous their output, that writers are ceasing to be distillers of quintessence and fast becoming 'forces of Nature'. This is superlatively the case with Balzac himself.

In July 1830 Charles X was driven from his throne. So ended a decade or more of vain attempts to obliterate 1789 and its consequences, to restore absolute monarchy, to reinstate the Church as the buttress of monarchy and the aristocracy as the dominant class, to emasculate Parliamentary institutions as defined by the 'Charter' of 1815 and stifle the Press. The 'three glorious days' of Revolution were the work of republicans—carbonari, Napoleonic veterans and working-men. Yet, thanks to the manoeuvres of skilful politicians, and by virtue of a carefully-conceived, more liberal Charter, Louis-Philippe, Duke of Orleans, stepped up to his cousin's throne as 'Roi des Français'. This elderly gentleman of ostentatiously simple tastes and family virtues seemed the very personification of constitutional government, a living guarantee of the 'liberty, equality and fraternity', whose revival the restored tricolor was meant to symbolize. But after a few months it became clear that no great change in the spirit of government had taken place. Although divine right had gone, Louis-Philippe did not intend to hand over effective rule to the well-to-do middle classes who in truth were, and who knew that they were, the backbone of the nation; and still less to the lower middle classes and the artisans. He and his successive ministers ignored the widespread demand for a vigorous defence of oppressed nations like Poland and Italy, and turned a deaf ear to appeals for electoral reform at home. The extension of the franchise, with universal suffrage as the ultimate goal, still looked like a panacea, both to ardent democrats and to the unfortunate 'prolétaires' (this word was now coming into current use) already suffering from the first effects of the industrial revolution, that change-over from rural and domestic craftmanship to the factory system which was to make sensible progress during the July Monarchy and to bring wage-slavery, unemployment, slums, squalor and starvation in its train. So Louis-Philippe, with his constant efforts to establish personal rule by patronage, management of elections and ministerial shufflings, pleased neither middle nor working classes, while a large part of the aristocracy adhered to 'legitimist' or 'Carlist' principles, that is to say, they remained faithful to the elder branch of the Bourbon dynasty.

From 1831 to 1836 the new King's position remained precarious; he improved it between 1836 and 1840 by resolute measures against Republicans and the Press. By 1840 his dynasty, although it only had a few more years to run, seemed to be fairly well established. His scurry into exile in 1848 was due more to social and economic than to political causes. Great as had been the advance in economic prosperity during his reign—the building of railways, the extension of banking and credit and the development of heavy industries —he and his ministries had done nothing to help the working classes. The Revolution of February 1848 resulted from collaboration between republican and socialist malcontents.

For the Monarchy of July was also the period when the challenge of socialism was first effectively heard: 'Romantic' socialism, as it is often called, because the emphasis it laid on ideal and spiritual values differentiates it so markedly from later brands, including Marxism, which were more positive, more class-conscious and more politically-minded. Again the year 1830 is a decisive date. Until his death in 1825 Claude-Henri de Saint-Simon had been laying the foundations of a scheme of social and industrial reorganization whose aim was, by the creation of something like what we should nowadays call a technocracy, to forestall the iniquities of a haphazardly-evolved capitalism and so promote the betterment of 'the poorest and most numerous class'. After 1825, Saint-Simon's disciples continued his work; it is interesting to observe that Balzac himself came into contact with some of them in May 1828, as the prospective printer of an ephemeral periodical, *Le Gymnase*, with which they were concerned. Within a short period Saint-Simonism grew into a school, then a sect, then a religion. Its leaders took note of the fact that 'man cannot live by bread alone', and that however wisely scientists, bankers and captains of industry—the king-pins of the future social hierarchy—may plan, they can achieve no results unless their efforts are supported, and even inspired, by moral enthusiasm and high ideals. Therefore in 1829 they founded the 'Saint-Simonian Church', in a well-meaning but absurd plagiarism of the Roman Church, with at first two 'Pères Suprêmes', then one alone at its head, and a hierarchy of 'apostles' and 'priests' who set out to preach their gospel by means of lectures, sermons, organized processions and quasi-religious manifestations. Before and after the July Revolution they roused, amused, shocked or disgusted the inhabitants of Paris by their eloquence, propaganda, fantastic costumes, masquerades and ceremonies.

However much they may have been derided, they brought to the attention of their contemporaries the urgency of social and economic questions, including that of the rights of women. Disputes about forms of government, they insisted, were by comparison of little importance. And by their appeals to all those 'hommes à sentiment' and 'hommes à imagination' whom they grouped together under the generic term 'artists', and to whom they were ready to assign a priestly and prophetic function in the new order, they did much to wean the leaders of the new literature from preoccupation with their individual selves or from devotion to a purely aesthetic purpose or creed. They awakened in them a sense, sometimes overwhelming, of their responsibility as privileged minds towards their fellow-creatures. The Saint-Simonian heyday soon passed, but the torch was taken over by other thinkers and sects: Charles Fourier, the founder of 'Phalansterian' co-operation; Pierre Leroux, the apostle of universal solidarity and the religion of humanity, and many others from Saint-Simon to Louis Blanc, Constantin Pecqueur and P.-J. Proudhon.

Balzac thus began his life-work in an atmosphere charged with new ideas. Great also was the contribution made to their fermentation by the disciples of illuminists like Saint-Martin and Swedenborg, or near-illuminists like Ballanche, or theocratic visionaries like Lamennais. The 'artist' was thereby acquiring a far more vivid sense of the vastness of his domain and the importance of his mission. The Saint-Simonian attack upon economic 'laissez-faire' sharpened the already critical attitude towards existing society taken up by the majority of Romantic writers, and Balzac is to be counted among them. The prevalent mood of literature therefore became, in its essence and its ultimate ideals, one of opposition and often of basic hostility to the régime. Before 1830, Romanticism had lagged behind political liberalism. After 1830, it far outstripped it. There is something of a revolutionary colouring (as regards religion, political or social outlook), in such works as *Notre-Dame de Paris*, *La Peau de chagrin*, *Indiana*, *Lélia*, *Stello*, *Chatterton*, *Les Chants du crépuscule*, *Jocelyn*, etc. Whatever his particular bias in politics, almost every writer was in spirit a critic and a rebel: Vigny with his strange mixture of pessimism and positivist optimism; Lamartine in his progress towards rational religion and republicanism; Hugo in his hesitant march towards socialism; Sand in her sentimental and religious utopianism, and Balzac too in his clamour for strong government and an efficient class-hierarchy. All set their faces against the rule of mediocrity (the 'juste milieu' of Louis-Philippe) and the worship of mammon.

For many writers, and notably for Balzac, this love of money was the cardinal vice of the middle class which since 1789 had gradually been imposing itself as the dominant element in the community. Hence their setting-up of the 'bourgeois' as a butt for mockery or attack. This Aunt Sally of the Romantic and future generations is represented as a gross individualist, strongly acquisitive, desiring only such a political régime as would allow him to amass his fortune and enjoy the power and consideration which the possession of money justifies; a Philistine in his attitude to literature and the arts; sceptical or interestedly conformist in religion; ruthless in his treatment of competitors and underlings; self-indulgent if not libertine once he has made his fortune. The foundations of this fortune have been laid in Imperial or Restoration times, and Balzac himself, who as the social historian of this century was to give rather more attention to the formative period, 1800–30, than to the following one, many times traced the career of this type of egoist, the personification and scourge of his age, and incarnated him in such characters as the banker Nucingen and the ex-perfumer Célestin Crevel. 'Comme on a raison d'avoir beaucoup d'argent!' exclaims the former. And the latter states the universal creed as follows:

Vous vous abusez, cher ange [he says to the guileless Baronne Hulot in *La cousine Bette*], si vous croyez que c'est le roi Louis-Philippe qui règne, et il ne s'abuse pas là-dessus. Il sait, comme nous tous, qu'au-dessus de la Charte il y a la sainte, la vénérée, la solide, l'aimable, la belle, la noble, la jeune, la toute-puissante pièce de cent sous!

Nucingen and Crevel are of course caricatures, and in any case represent only a section of the vast middle class, so infinite in its gradations, so heterogeneous in its composition. The ambitions of the higher type of 'bourgeois' went far beyond the accumulation of five-franc pieces. There were the middle-class land-owners who sought to acquire the status of the aristocrats they had displaced; the intellectuals like Guizot, Rémusat and Villemain who used University chairs as stepping-stones to ministerial careers; the civil servants and lawyers of all varieties and grades whose aim in life was to reach higher rank by whatever means came to hand; the newspaper-owners, editors and journalists who wormed or bludgeoned their way to influence and wealth by misusing the power of the Press. According to Balzac, there was one guiding principle at work in all these spheres of activity: 'Ôte-toi de là que je m'y mette!'; and the well-stocked portrait-gallery of the 'Comédie Humaine' bears witness to the close scrutiny he gave to the climbers of his age. But the money-making community was to be at once the object of his envy and the target for his main attack.

Not that he too severely castigated the relatively honest merchant who produces or handles goods, such as César Birotteau and his lieutenant Anselme Popinot, or the Lebas family of cloth-merchants in *La Maison du chat qui pelote*: men who as a rule had no higher objective than social prestige in their Paris quarter, possession of the Cross of the Legion of Honour, officer-rank in the National Guard and a comfortable income on retirement. These he treated with good humour or sympathy, for he was not a socialist. In his eyes the reign of money meant the reign of bankers, brokers, jobbers, discounters, speculators and money-lenders of all sorts, who exploited the needs or embarrassments of others. 'Les affaires, c'est bien simple, c'est l'argent des autres.' This aphorism, which the younger Dumas was to put into the mouth of a typical speculator a few years after Balzac's death, sums up a situation which, much as we must allow for exaggeration and even obsession on Balzac's part, was prevalent enough to stamp the Louis-Philippe period, in so far as the daily business of bread-winning is concerned, as one of rapacity. How strange the contrast between this basic materialism and the lofty and effusive idealism which distinguishes so much of the thought and literature of the period, between the earth-bound stolidity of the many and the aerial soarings of the few!

Paris and the provinces were tarred with the same brush. But Paris was the chief battle-ground in the 'struggle for life', the scramble after gold and pleasure, which Balzac was to depict. On Paris his attention was mainly to be focused. A city of light and shade, of elegance and squalor, the centre of social brilliance, the home of the intelligentsia, the hub of the artistic universe, the goal of the ambitious, the Mecca of the provincial, the witches' cauldron of political and administrative intrigue, the thieves' kitchen of financiers and speculators. Until its transformation by Haussmann under Napoleon III, it still remained largely an overgrown medieval city, insanitary and insalubrious through the crudity of its sewage system and the inadequacy of its water-supply; a medley of styles and centuries, with its multiplicity of dirty and tortuous streets clustered round imposing buildings and historic monuments. To its more elegant quarters, the Faubourg Saint-Germain, stretching southwards from the Quai d'Orsay on the left bank of the Seine, and the Faubourg Saint Honoré in the Champs-Élysées region, Balzac was to give little descriptive attention, however much he might glorify the former, where the old aristocracy had their mansions, as the pinnacle of social attainment.

He was indeed more fascinated by the older and more crowded districts: the Latin Quarter and the Île de la Cité, and, on the right bank of the Seine, the squalid and populous regions neighbouring on the Louvre, the Hôtel de Ville, the Halles; and above all the once fashionable quarters of the Marais and the Temple, where the professional and middle classes were now largely congregated. These and the Chaussée d'Antin region, the domain of banking and commerce, and the centres of amusement, pleasure and vice, like the purlieus of the Palais-Royal and the Tuileries, and the boulevards east of the Rue de la Paix, excited much of his descriptive verve. In particular he minutely scrutinized the dowdy streets and their decrepit, grimy houses; in general he regarded the city as a Dantesque inferno. 'Là, tout s'évapore, s'éteint, se rallume, étincelle, pétille et se consume.' The 'grand monstre moderne' which he loved and execrated was changing perceptibly, but was not to be altered beyond recognition while he was busy perpetuating the memory of its quaint and sordid corners in anticipation of future metamorphoses. In truth it was scarcely monstrous by comparison with the metropolis of to-day. It was still relatively small, studded and surrounded as it was with green or vacant spaces. But even while he was writing, the incipient industrial revolution was sucking the rural population into the capital. The population of Paris in 1831 was 785,000; in 1848 it had risen to 1,053,000.

ii. Balzac and the *beau monde*

According to *Victor Hugo raconté par un témoin de sa vie*, Balzac sided with the Romantics at the first night of *Hernani*. This did not prevent him from writing scathing reviews of the play, or from scoffing, from first to last, at the 'childish stupidity' of Hugo's dramas. None the less, he was very much in the main literary swim from then onwards. His status scarcely permitted him as yet to treat on equal terms with literary celebrities like Lamartine, Vigny and Hugo, but he was friendly with Charles Nodier and recognized a kindred spirit in Stendhal. He knew Alexandre Dumas, and probably disliked him already. The painter Auguste Borget, a friend of Zulma Carraud, and for several years a stalwart friend of Balzac, introduced him to George Sand when, in 1831, she left her husband in Berri to set up house on the Quai Saint-Michel with her fellow-countryman and lover, Jules Sandeau. Sand herself has written with enthusiasm of Balzac's frequent visits, and of their 'camaraderie', only temporarily interrupted in 1833 when she quarrelled with Sandeau and Balzac took his part.

Among the lesser lights of his acquaintance, in addition to Latouche who, as he became more friendly with Sand, became less so with Balzac, were Eugène Sue, Philarète Chasles, Jules Janin, and Paul Lacroix. Sue was a former naval surgeon who was to make his fortune, much to Balzac's disgust, by badly-written sensational novels. Chasles, an old acquaintance of 'Lord R'Hoone' days, was shortly to write a preface for the *Romans et Contes philosophiques* (1831) and join with him and Charles Rabou in writing a volume of short stories, *Contes bruns* (1832). Janin was the author of two macabre novels, one of which, *L'Âne mort et la femme guillotinée*, Balzac parodied in *Le Voleur*. As critic of the *Journal des Débats*, Janin took ample revenge in later years. Paul Lacroix wrote historical novels under the pseudonym of 'P.-L. Jacob, Bibliophile'. He too came to realize how sharp a pen Balzac wielded when writing reviews.

Balzac also rubbed shoulders with talented draughtsmen and cartoonists, Henri Monnier, Gavarni, Tony Johannot, Charles Philipon, Honoré Daumier, Charlet and Grandville, many of whom were before long to be busy illustrating his works. He knew the composer Berlioz and got on well with Rossini. And he had fluctuating relations with newspaper directors, Victor Ratier of *La Silhouette*, the affluent Dr Véron of *Le Constitutionel*, that indefatigable founder of periodicals Émile de Girardin, the versatile and unscrupulous Victor Bohain who in 1833 started *L'Europe Littéraire*, and those two prickly editors, Amédée Pichot of *La Revue de Paris* and François Buloz of *La Revue des deux Mondes*.

Balzac's penetration into smart Parisian society began in the winter of 1829–30. He first gained access to the predominantly literary and artistic salons; but it had long been a tradition in the 'beau monde parisien' that nobility, elegance and literature should be equally well represented at their 'raouts' and soirées. His first hostesses were ladies renowned for beauty and social talents under the Directory, Consulate and Empire. According to *Balzac mis à nu*, Balzac's initial social successes were with the Doumerc set at Versailles, where the Duchesse d'Abrantès had been living since 1821, and he had got to know both her and Sophie Gay through them. Mme d'Abrantès was tired of Versailles by 1828, and moved to a suite of rooms in the Augustinian convent of L'Abbaye-aux-Bois at Paris, which lodged other illustrious women who liked to have one foot in the cloister provided that they could keep the other firmly planted in mundane society. Here resided the famous Juliette Récamier, wife of a rich banker of the Chaussée d'Antin, and formerly a friend of Mme de Staël, who had shared with her the experience of incurring Napoleon's displeasure as fomenters of intrigue. Mme Récamier had been an outstanding social figure since Imperial times; now she was the intimate friend of Chateaubriand, the scientist J.-J. Ampère, and the amiable dreamer Ballanche. Probably Mme d'Abrantès introduced Balzac to her.

He also began to frequent the Paris salon of Mme Sophie Gay, a beautiful 'merveilleuse' in Directory days, whose social prestige had increased during the Restoration. She herself was a novelist, and wrote the gossip column in *La Mode*, which her future son-in-law, Émile de Girardin, founded in 1829. She had two charming and talented daughters, Élise, married to Comte O'Donnell, and Delphine, a young writer of occasional verse, who married Émile de Girardin in 1831, and became one of the most brilliant hostesses of Paris. For many years Balzac was to be a welcome and intimate guest with both mother and daughters. Another salon which he now frequented was that of the painter Baron Gérard, who received not only social celebrities, but also such eminent artists as Gros, Delacroix, the brothers Devéria, the sculptor David d'Angers (who in 1843 made a bust of Balzac), and the caricaturist Gavarni. He also welcomed such prominent thinkers and writers as Cuvier, Nodier, Stendhal, Mérimée, Vigny, Hugo, Loève-Weimars, the translator of Hoffmann, and that very Hoffmannesque creature, Dr Koreff, the notorious 'magnetiser', whom Balzac grew to hate in later years, but who must have fascinated him at first. Baron Gérard's salon is said to have provided the model for the one Balzac described in the *Conversation entre onze heures et minuit* which he contributed to *Contes bruns*.

Vous trouverez ailleurs en Europe, d'élégantes manières, de la cordialité, de la bonhomie, de la science; mais à Paris seulement, dans ce salon et quelques autres encore, se rencontre l'esprit particulier qui donne à toutes ces qualités sociales un agréable et capricieux ensemble, je ne sais quelle allure fluviale qui fait facilement serpenter cette profusion de pensées, de formules, de contes, de documens historiques. Paris, capitale du goût, connaît seul cette science qui change une conversation en une joute, où chaque nature d'esprit se condense par un trait, où chacun dit sa phrase et jette son expérience dans un mot, où tout le monde s'amuse, se délasse, et s'exerce.

In such company Balzac sometimes made a distasteful impression, especially on squeamish persons like Vigny, Fontaney and Delacroix. He was full of verve and gaiety, had remarkably fine eyes and a jovial laugh. But he had no idea of personal fastidiousness or of quiet elegance in dress. His very exuberance must often have jarred on sensitive nerves. In fact he was something of a jay in peacock's feathers, and he himself wrote of the embarrassment he felt and the humiliation he suffered when making his first invasion of Parisian society.[1] But invade it he did. And he

[1] A phrase in *La Duchesse de Langeais*, where he comments on 'l'infertilité des salons, leur vide, leur peu de profondeur, et la répug-

found his way, not only into the set of intellectuals, artists and men of letters, but also into more purely fashionable centres. The author of the scandalous *Physiologie du mariage* and the *Scènes de la vie privée* aroused the curiosity of established hostesses anxious to fill their salons with interesting people; women now forgotten, but socially powerful in their day: Mme Hamelin, the 'languid creole', Comtesse Merlin, who is supposed to have provided Balzac with a model for Mme Schontz in *Béatrix,* and Princess Bagration, widow of the general who figures in Tolstoy's *War and Peace*, a former mistress of Metternich, and one of the most brilliant society leaders in Vienna during the Congress of 1814–15. Here, as in the salon of Mme Récamier, Balzac met politicians, scientists and scholars, and an imposing array of dukes and duchesses, counts and countesses bearing the most brilliant names of the Faubourg Saint-Germain. 'Toute la gloire et tout le charme de la France étaient là,' says Lamartine of Mme Récamier's salon. Here in July 1831 Balzac gave a reading of *La Peau de chagrin*, and it became quite usual for him to tell stories at Sophie Gay's receptions, at Baron Gérard's musical evenings, and, later, in Delphine de Girardin's drawing-room. A skit he wrote for *La Caricature* in December 1830[1] indicates that he had recently been present at one of those readings for which Charles Nodier's salon at the Arsenal had become famous.

The Parisian 'monde' was not exclusive or snobbish, within certain limits. It could not even be termed respectable in a narrow sense, for respectability has never been a conspicuous social virtue in France. Many of the ladies who welcomed Balzac had dubious incidents in their past, but

nance que les gens supérieurs éprouvent à faire le méchant commerce d'y échanger leurs pensées', is perhaps an expression of this embarrassment. Conard, XIII, 287.

[1] *Les Litanies romantiques*, Conard, *O. D.*, II, 217.

were obviously not ostracized on that account. Such great aristocrats as the Duc de Duras and the Duc de Fitz-James, with whom Balzac was soon to become friendly, were no more averse than journalist-dandies like Lautour-Mézeray from spending an evening in the salon of the demi-mondaine, Olympe Pélissier, at present the mistress of Eugène Sue, and later to become the mistress and then the wife of the composer Rossini. In the early thirties Balzac too had his entrée there and, if report be true, would not have objected to supplanting Sue. In *La Peau de chagrin*, the hero, Raphaël de Valentin, hides one night in the bedroom of the cold-hearted Fœdora to witness her toilette: Pichot avers that Balzac had made the same experiment in Olympe's flat. Balzac also got to know some prominent bankers of the period, James de Rothschild, whose wife, according to the Comtesse d'Agoult, was a woman of superlative charm and distinction, and Baron Aguado, a generous Amphitryon who gave dinners to a mixed concourse of writers, dancers and courtesans, bearing no doubt some resemblance to the orgy likewise recorded in *La Peau de chagrin*. And Balzac's life would have been incomplete if he had not visited the more expensive cafés—the Café de Paris, the Café Procope, the Café Hardi, the Rocher de Cancale and Tortoni's restaurant: resorts of 'viveurs', dandies, elegant roisterers and practical jokers, among whom was more than a sprinkling of writers and journalists.

And so, from now on, Honoré Balzac has become Honoré *de* Balzac. He has promoted himself to armorial bearings—approximately those of the Balzacs d'Entragues. He has ample opportunity to mix with, observe and appraise the Parisian élite. Did this give him enough social experience to portray the life and manners of lords and ladies, as he so often attempted to do in the 'Comédie Humaine'?

Apparently it did, in so far at least as the façade is concerned. Could meetings and conversations with them at parties offer him scope for the understanding of their inner selves, dissembled under a mask of social promiscuity and fictitious cordiality? Had he the delicacy of perception, the subtlety of intuition required for such a task? These questions have been diversely answered by modern critics. Few of Balzac's contemporaries challenged the truth of the picture he gave. Sainte-Beuve, although he was unremittingly hostile to Balzac, admitted it.[1] For us, perhaps, Balzac's most characteristic short-coming in posing his social celebrities is his inability to disguise from his readers the snobbish pleasure it gave him to tell them how the truly distinguished behave and converse.[2] But a graver question occurs to the mind: was the 'beau monde' from which he drew his models perfectly representative of the Faubourg Saint-Germain in particular and the French aristocracy in general?[3] Was not the truest part of the latter also the quietest, living in formal simplicity, nursing the virtues and courtliness traditional to it, and eschewing that social brilliance and promiscuity which obtained then, as it always obtains, all the publicity that writers of memoirs and gossip-columnists can confer? Has the history of this real French aristocracy, which still exists, ever been written? Balzac often did more

[1] *Causeries du Lundi*, IX, 327–8, commenting on the disadvantage from which Stendhal suffered in that respect.

[2] See Proust's amusing reflexions on this subject in the unedited fragment published in *La Table Ronde*, July 1950, and given the title 'Les Personnages de Balzac'.

[3] The Comtesse d'Agoult ('Daniel Stern'), in *Mes Souvenirs, 1806–1833*, emphasizes the exclusiveness of the genuinely old aristocracy during the Restoration, and also the rigidity of their social habits. After July 1830 they closed their ranks still further for a time and went into a sort of social mourning. But soon some great ladies, like the Duchesse de Rauzun, the Marquise de la Bourdonnaye and Mme de La Grange, felt that they were missing too much and opened their salons to 'des personnes nouvelles', including literary and artistic 'parvenus' (3rd edition, 1880, p. 337 sqq.).

than hint at its existence. He perhaps drew closest to it in his sketch of the Marquis d'Espard in *L'Interdiction*, of the d'Esgrignons in *Le Cabinet des antiques*, of the Du Guénic family in *Béatrix*.

iii. Journalism: politics: Henriette de Castries

It was by no means certain in 1830 that Balzac was to apply himself undeviatingly to the writing of novels. A journalistic career was opening out to him. New periodicals were being founded in abundance since 1829: short-lived ones as a rule, thanks to the rapidity with which they fell foul of authority, vehicles for lambent wit (or what passed as such), caricatures, personal and political attacks. There were more serious and more permanent ventures such as the *Revue de Paris* and the *Revue des deux Mondes*. The *Feuilleton des Journaux politiques*, which Balzac, under the aegis of Émile de Girardin, seems practically to have run himself, was serious enough. Some of its reviews were even markedly Saint-Simonian in tone; but it lasted only from March to July 1830. He was well paid for his newspaper work and was able thereby to begin reducing his debt to his mother. There was thus a temptation to fritter away talent and to settle down to literary parasitism, like the journalists of the 'Comédie Humaine'—Émile Blondet, Étienne Lousteau, Claude Vignon, etc. But although he was to spend three energetic years working for the 'petits journaux', such a vocation was scarcely fitted to one of his vigorous creative temperament.

A stronger temptation assailed him during his period of free-lance journalism. By turning his pen to more serious topics, he could hope to prove his mettle as a politician. The moment seemed favourable for this, since the Revolution of

July, like all political upheavals, gave the signal for a scramble for places and honours. As Charles X trundled into exile, those who by political journalism had helped to displace him had promptly stepped forward to claim a reward. Balzac had spent the summer of 1830 with Mme de Berny, living at the enchanting cottage of La Grenadière near Tours, and then taking a trip down the Loire into Brittany. He was wandering on the banks of the Indre when the news of the 'Three Glorious Days' came to him. He was fairly indifferent at first. He had not made himself conspicuous or tiresome by political innuendo or satire; he was too young to stand for election as a deputy (until the new electoral law reduced the age of eligibility from forty to thirty), and too indigent to satisfy the property qualification, even when that in its turn was reduced. But circumstances arose which turned his diffidence into ambition, and for several years diverted him from complete devotion to his true vocation.

Émile de Girardin invited him to contribute a series of 'Lettres sur Paris' to *Le Voleur*, which he had founded in 1828. These letters were intended to be of general interest, but naturally the political interest was paramount. Balzac returned to Paris and started the series on September 20th. He also joined with Charles Philipon in launching *La Caricature*, a weekly intended for humour and social satire but which, like its forerunners, *La Mode* and *La Silhouette*, quickly acquired a political hue. It distinguished itself by its ridicule of Louis-Philippe and the 'juste milieu' party, and during the two years that Balzac wrote for it, it was often prosecuted and once suspended. But it was the 'Lettres sur Paris' that Balzac used in order to voice his evolving political opinions. The sympathetic expectancy he showed at first gave way to disgust with the inertia and flabbiness of the new régime, and to lamentation over the fact that 'gérontocratie', the government of old men which he thought characteristic of the previous reign, still continued. His attitude is that of a disgruntled liberal, contemptuous of an effete aristocracy, but paying no homage to democratic mysticism. The aim of government, he avers, is to keep the masses under control whilst supplying their needs and giving them a modicum of enlightenment; it is also to guarantee the well-to-do in the stable possession of their property. The anti-religious and anti-legitimist riots of 14–15 February 1831, when the mob sacked the church and presbytery of Saint-Germain-l'Auxerrois and the palace of the Archbishop of Paris, served to convince him of the weakness of the government, but also revealed the danger of anticlericalism. In April he published a brochure: *Enquête sur la politique des deux ministères* signed 'de Balzac, électeur éligible'. The views he expressed were really those he was always to hold: the need for a strong head of the State, a monied middle-class to provide a legislative assembly whose function would be to vote supplies and to assent to, rather than control legislation, an effective aristocracy to act as a buffer between King and people; in brief a well-defined social and political hierarchy.

The evolution in Balzac's thought from this position to the adoption by the end of 1831 of the legitimist slogan 'Dieu et le Roi' has been minutely examined in M. Guyon's thesis: *La Pensée politique et sociale de Balzac*.[1] In early 1831 Balzac was looking about him to find a constituency likely to accept him as parliamentary candidate, possibly Fougères, Tours or Cambrai. Hoping to acquire the necessary property qualification by marriage to a young heiress, Éléonore de Trumilly, he left it to his mother and sister to make the necessary overtures to her family. Enquiries about

[1] Armand Colin, 1947.

the political situation at Fougères and Tours gave discouraging results; at Cambrai he had only a friendly journalist, S. H. Berthoud, to assess his chances. It became plain to him that a stranger and a non-party man was not likely to be elected.

The decision he then took—to champion the Church and Legitimate Monarchy—is consistent with the general trend of his thought, though personal motives also played their part. Mme de Berny had no respect for legitimism; Zulma Carraud was an ardent liberal; the Duchesse d'Abrantès no doubt fostered his secret Bonapartist leanings. But the royalism of the Trumilly family probably counted for something in his 'conversion' to legitimism. More important still was a new sentimental relationship which brought him into legitimist circles and confirmed in him that sympathy for the principle of aristocracy which was part and parcel of his sensitivity or, perhaps, of his conceit as an artist enamoured of luxury and elegance.

In October 1831, while Balzac was making one of his frequent sojourns with the Margonnes at Saché, he received from a supposed Englishwoman a letter in which appreciation of his talent was mingled with sharp reproaches for his treatment of women in *La Physiologie du mariage* and the recently published *Peau de chagrin*. He defended himself in guarded but eloquent terms. The following February she disclosed her true identity and proposed a meeting; she was the Marquise (later Duchesse) de Castries, of unimpeachably aristocratic rank, descended through her mother from the royal race of the Stuarts. By May 1832 he was paying her almost daily visits, and they were on terms of 'tender and devoted friendship'. But he wished to take matters further. He was fascinated by her charm and attentiveness, flattered by the idea of having a marquise for a mistress, and hoping to find in her a second Mme de Berny, one who was 'jeune et plus à même de me servir', as he candidly told his sister later on. Who shall say in what proportion such motives were mixed? In any case he was caught in the toils, and longed for the ecstasy which the ultimate favours of Henriette de Castries could give him.

This lady,[1] emancipated like most of Balzac's highly-born acquaintances, had long lived apart from her husband. The great event of her life had been her passion for Victor Metternich, son of the Austrian Chancellor. He had died of consumption in 1828, leaving her a son Roger who was the apple of her eye. She lived in comparative seclusion, since a fall from a horse in the hunting-field had caused an injury to her spine, and made her almost a cripple. This was a good reason, more decisive perhaps than her loyalty to her dead lover's memory, for her wishing to keep her romance with Balzac on the spiritual plane. But she has often passed for a heartless coquette for encouraging a passion which she refused to satisfy, although there is much in her subsequent correspondence with him to show that she was really fond of him. At all events, from March to September 1832 the sentiment between them refined into warm affection on her part and passionate ardour on his side. He called her 'Marie', for the name had tender associations since he had first used it for Laure d'Abrantès, to distinguish her from his sister and Laure de Berny.

She was the niece of the Duc de Fitz-James, now, with Berryer, one of the most active leaders of the legitimist party. They had succeeded in weaning the legitimists from their childish policy of passive resistance to the new regime, and had persuaded them to form an active party with a constructive programme and a newspaper to support it—*Le*

[1] For the history of her relations with Balzac, see M. Bouteron, *Cahiers balzaciens*, No. 6.

Rénovateur, founded by Laurentie. Probably Balzac had already met Fitz-James in the salon of Olympe Pélissier, but Mme de Castries brought them closer together. They soon became cordial friends. Balzac declared his adherence to their legitimist programme and became a contributor, early in 1832, to *Le Rénovateur*.

As he told Zulma Carraud, he wanted the abolition of all nobility except an hereditary Chamber of Peers. He wanted the French Clergy to be freed from Roman domination at a time when gallicanism was at a low ebb and ultramontanism a rising tide. He wanted France to take possession of her 'natural frontiers', which would have meant war. He wanted a regime in which real superiority of talent would be recognized and rewarded by promotion into the higher social grades. He wanted economy in national expenditure, better management of the public purse, and a measure of education for all. One of his first demands of the legitimists, in his articles of May and June 1832, was that they should renounce their isolationism, take the oath to the existing Charter, and frankly enter the political arena. He thought of standing for Chinon as a legitimist candidate; but a fall from his carriage in May immobilized him for some time, and made an electioneering campaign impossible. Perhaps he shrank from the thought of starting one. At any rate, the slender chance of winning the seat at Chinon was lost.

If the legitimists were glad to enlist him as a talented writer, he in turn meant to use them to further his ambitions, and he earned the displeasure both of Mme de Berny and of the severe Zulma for such 'Machiavellism'. He still had to obtain his property qualification, and by now was thinking of persuading a rich widow—Baronne Caroline Deurbroucq—to marry him. He had met her the previous autumn, and hoped to settle the matter while on holiday at

Saché in June; but legal affairs prevented her from coming to Tours to see him. He grew tired of waiting and left Saché in July for the Carrauds' new home, the powder-factory near Angoulême. Mme de Castries was at Aix-les-Bains and pressing him to join her there. Both ambition and desire were drawing him towards her, and Zulma Carraud, though disapproving of the whole affair, advised him to go. He arrived at Aix towards the end of August, and spent September with Mme de Castries, intent upon overcoming her resistance. He found her kind, but still firm. They visited beauty-spots together, the Lac du Bourget and the Grande-Chartreuse, where the idea for a novel, *Le Médecin de campagne*, came to him. She and her uncle had arranged to go to Italy, and he was invited to accompany them. He accepted, and they got as far as Geneva. There matters came to a head. No precise details are known, but evidently 'Marie' refused to carry familiarity with him farther than the kiss she had already allowed him. Bruised, angry, humiliated, he left her and retreated to La Bouleaunière to regain calm in the saddened but still soothing company of Mme de Berny.

How much was Balzac's fury and dejection at what he regarded as a cold betrayal due to thwarted passion or to wounded vanity? He certainly dramatized the affair, and for years to come, in correspondence with sympathetic female friends, he did not hesitate to recall his rôle of disappointed lover. The effects of this set-back on his sentimental life and literary work will be considered later. How did it affect his political intentions? Did he conclude, as Mme de Berny and Zulma Carraud had independently surmised (these two friends of Balzac never met), that Fitz-James and his party had been using Henriette de Castries as a bait without intending that he should be allowed to swallow it? At all events, he was not so petty-minded as to shed his new-found convictions for personal motives. He continued his friendship with Fitz-James, who, in September 1833, offered to reimburse him for the losses he suffered in his lawsuit with the editor, Mame. And he continued his collaboration with the party.

But his political writings betrayed more and more clearly the divergence between their principles and his. An article he wrote in September 1832 for *Le Rénovateur* entitled 'Du Gouvernement moderne' was never printed in that journal. As an attack on constitutional government and a defence of the Bourbons it could have pleased the legitimists, although they would have knit their brows as they read that 'la Légitimité, toute absurde qu'elle puisse paraître, serait un principe à inventer s'il n'existait pas'. A man whose plea for monarchy was founded on political expediency, and not on respect for divine right, was a dangerous and uncomfortable auxiliary. Perhaps he did not himself realize how distasteful his views were becoming to the aristocratic party. A literary periodical sponsored by the legitimists, *L'Écho de la Jeune France*, was founded in the spring of 1833. The only contribution he made to it was the first two chapters of what was afterwards to be called *La Duchesse de Langeais*. The second of these was a dissertation on the Faubourg Saint-Germain and the shortcomings of the French aristocracy—its egoism, irresponsibility, and inefficiency as a leaven in French politics and French society.

During all this time he had *Le Médecin de campagne* on the stocks. This was a work conceived in white-hot enthusiasm and probably dashed off in its earliest form in a few days, but subsequently so revised and expanded as to become a complete profession of faith. When at last it came out in September 1833, this tale of a benevolent doctor who retires to 'un gros bourg situé entre Grenoble et la Grande Chartreuse' (generally taken to be Voreppe), and devotes himself to the regeneration and prosperity of its inhabitants, turned out to be a vehicle for political, social and religious propaganda. It contains all that Balzac had been minded to say in *Le Rénovateur* against the parliamentary system and representative government. It also gave him his first opportunity to define the part which the Catholic religion is called upon to play in society as a restraining force, a moral influence, and a bond giving unity and fraternity to the whole community. At the same time this novel shows him in his true political colours. It reveals the persistence in his mind of certain liberal principles as regards administration and economic life. It shows that legitimism for him had only been a means to an end, a *pis aller* even. What Balzac still looked for was the man of genius who should be the natural leader of his people. The cult of Napoleon that the book fosters, and the stimulus to the Napoleonic legend which certain scenes and characters provide, prove plainly that another 'man of destiny', whatever his origin, would have been more welcome to Balzac than a ready-made Bourbon, however galvanized and refurbished he might be.

Balzac had by now thought out for himself a complete and coherent system, but it could have no appeal to the legitimists. Their newspapers attacked the book, their leaders turned away from him, and Fitz-James soon reverted to intransigent Carlism. And so Balzac gave up the idea of an immediate political career, although the urge to become a statesman returned from time to time in later years. In the meantime, in spite of love-affairs, the distractions of dandyism, quarrels with publishers and editors, and political manoeuvres, he had found time to produce about 250 articles and reviews in a dozen periodicals, more 'Scenes of

Private Life' and several editions of *Romans et Contes philosophiques*. He had published one of his most fascinating novels, *La Peau de chagrin*. He had laid the foundations of his 'Scenes of Parisian Life' in what is now known as *Le colonel Chabert*, in *Ferragus* and in the as yet unfinished *Duchesse de Langeais*. He had found his way towards the 'Scenes of Provincial Life' with *Le Curé de Tours*, had published the first version of *Louis Lambert*, half autobiographical, half metaphysical, and, by way of contrast, two volumes of his Rabelaisian extravaganzas, *Les Contes drolatiques*. He had satisfied himself, in writing *Le Médecin de campagne*, of his power to make the form of the novel serve as well for the expression of ideas—'ce qu'il [Napoleon] n'a pu achever par l'épée, je l'accomplirai par la plume'— as for the portrayal of manners and the entertainment of an eager reading public. The impassioned monsters of *Eugénie Grandet*, *La Recherche de l'absolu* and *Le père Goriot*—the rapacious miser, the crazy alchemist, the idolatrous father— were beginning to take shape within his brain, which was also seething with schemes for an all-embracing system of 'Social Studies'. He was on the brink of his exciting discovery that, when a novel was finished and the characters had played their parts in it, they need not be consigned to oblivion, but could be brought in again to play other parts in other novels, and so give a fascinating impression of reality to the world his imagination was creating. Hence his famous innovation 'le retour des personnages'. The year 1833 saw the end of his collaboration with such flighty journals as *La Caricature* and such short-lived ones as *L'Europe Littéraire*. Henceforth, in the main, the periodical press was merely to constitute a means for making an additional profit, or to provide a repository for his novels and stories before they were published in book-form.

iv. 'L'Étrangère'

It is easy to exaggerate the part involuntarily played by Henriette de Castries in bringing Balzac to the point of renouncing a political career. The shock of his disillusionment with her had more important repercussions. In October 1832, in order to punish the proud lady for having trifled with him, he composed for insertion in *Le Médecin de campagne* the famous 'Confession inédite', whose ostensible purpose was to furnish the brilliant young doctor Benassis with a resounding motive for leaving Paris and burying himself in the Dauphiné. This unfinished 'Confession' bears comparison with *René*, *Obermann* and *Adolphe*, those outstanding products of the 'maladie du siècle', as the typically Romantic elegy of a soul whose superiority plunges him into a void of spiritual solitude which, in this case, a woman unaccountably refuses to fill. To this personal effusion Balzac consigned his grievance against Henriette.

Elle a joué avec un sentiment vrai, avec une vie entière, sans remords aucun. . . . Pourquoi m'a-t-elle nommé pendant quelques jours son bien-aimé, si elle devait me ravir ce titre, le seul dont le cœur se soucie? Elle a tout confirmé par un baiser, cette suave et sainte promesse que, par une distinction spéciale, Dieu nous a laissée en souvenir des cieux. . . .

And he describes the Geneva crisis thus, without being able to explain the lady's sudden *volte-face*:

La veille, j'étais tout pour elle, le lendemain, je n'étais plus rien . . . pendant la nuit, une femme était morte: c'était celle que j'aimais . . . elle m'offrait, suivant l'exécrable coutume des femmes de bonne compagnie, son amitié. Mais, accepter son amitié, c'était l'absoudre de son crime.[1]

Le Médecin de campagne hung fire, so much so that

[1] These quotations are taken from Bernard Guyon's edition of the 'Confession inédite', in *La Création littéraire chez Balzac*, Armand Colin, 1951.

Mame, the publisher to whom he had sold it, lost patience, and in the summer of 1833 brought a successful action against him for breach of contract. In the meantime, on his return to Paris at the end of 1832, instead of revealing his discomfiture to a derisive world by means of the 'Confession', he decided to avenge himself on Henriette by telling the story of Antoinette de Langeais in *Ne touchez pas la hache*, whose title was later changed to *La Duchesse de Langeais*. This novel relates how a beautiful and intelligent but cold-hearted and coquettish fashionable lady of the Faubourg Saint-Germain denies to her lover, General de Montriveau, what Henriette de Castries had refused to Balzac. She is brought by his threatened brutality to realize the enormity of her crime, repents of it too late, and spends the rest of her life expiating it in a convent.

Since Balzac was thus free to vent his spleen in *Ne touchez pas la hache*, the lamentations and vituperations of the 'Confession inédite' became superfluous. Because he was warming up to the evangelizing purpose of *Le Médecin de campagne*, and because after all Dr Benassis' failure to seduce a married woman was not the most edifying of preludes to the rôle of 'good shepherd' which Benassis was to take over, Balzac replaced it by another confession, according to which his withdrawal from society was motivated by the loss of a dearly-loved though illegitimate son, and the refusal of a perfectly respectable girl to cast in her lot with his. As for *Ne touchez pas la hache*, it remained unfinished until early 1834, by which time Balzac was involved in a more lasting love-affair.

From 1831 to 1832 he was beginning to receive what amounted to a 'fan-mail': three or four letters a day—so he tells Zulma Carraud—from adoring, admiring or indignant women, whose veil of anonymity he occasionally succeeded in tearing away.[1] So began also the relationship with the nobly-born Polish countess Evelina Rzewuska, wife of an elderly, rich, feudal landowner in the Ukraine, Wenceslas Hanski, himself of old family, though less illustrious than hers. They lived at Wierzchownia, in a vast palace in the midst of the steppes. Evelina was in all probability only nineteen months younger than Balzac:[2] a lively, intelligent, temperamental woman with some claim to beauty, inclined to the cultivated sensibility of her era, latently sensual and emotionally religious. Underneath all this was a fair stock of common sense. She was an avid reader of French Romantic literature. Her husband was amiable, cultured, but dull, and she was bored with her life as a chatelaine ruling over a large community of serfs and domestics. On February 28th, 1832, Balzac's publisher, Gosselin, handed him a letter signed 'L'Étrangère'. It contained the first advances from her who was to become Balzac's *princesse lointaine*. It was to be followed by others, but only two of them are extant—the letters of an intellectually and emotionally starved woman who, in her remote domain, yearned for the brilliance and variety of French culture. She was reading Balzac's stories as they reached her, and expressed in extravagant terms her telepathic, platonic and mystic sympathy with the author of her choice.

Enchanting vistas were thus revealed to Balzac after his disappointment with Mme de Castries. It was not until December 1832 that he was able to respond, at her request, by a message inserted in *La Quotidienne*. Thus began a

---

[1] M. Bouteron has collected some of them in *Cahiers balzaciens*, III and IV.

[2] Sophie de Korwin-Piotrowska, in *Balzac et le monde slave* (Honoré Champion, 1933), p. 20, note I, surmises that she was born on 24th December 1800, according to the Russian calendar, which means 5th January 1801, according to our Gregorian calendar.

voluminous correspondence which continued, with inter-
missions, until October 1848, when Balzac rejoined his now
widowed Ève, as he called her, at her castle of Wierzchownia,
never to be parted from her again until death. Nearly all Ève's
letters to Balzac were destroyed at her command by him in
September 1847, or by herself after his death. But those of
Balzac to her have been preserved and edited in four large
volumes, covering the period January 1833 to September
1847.[1] Even more than his published correspondence with
his family, Mme de Berny, Mme de Castries and Mme
Carraud, they form an invaluable document, not only for
the history of his work, but more so still for the revelation
they give of Balzac the man and the lover.

What had these two to write about at the outset? Her
object was, while laying bare her Romantic soul, to comment
on his works with an enthusiasm that undoubtedly warmed
his heart, though also, sometimes, with a note of criticism
when her Slavonic temperament was not perfectly satisfied
with his insight into the mysteries of feminine psychology.
His object was to explain and defend his works, to unfold
his plans and ambitions, to expand upon his financial
struggles, the magnitude of his task, and the single-minded
devotion he gave to it. Also to make love, for in the first few
months Balzac's ardour waxed with almost every letter.

It is easy to understand his state of mind, in spite of the
fundamental absurdity of a love-drama inspired by a woman
he had never met, and of whose name and status he was still
imperfectly aware. Early in 1832 Mme de Berny's generous
self-effacement had enabled him to put his relationship with
her on a basis of platonic friendship. Love-making with the
Duchesse d'Abrantès was a thing of the past. That he had

[1] Those he wrote after that date are not yet collected in a volume, but
selections of them were published in the *Revue de Paris*, November
1948, August 1950 and August 1952. This last volume is in preparation.

other affairs is indicated by a letter he wrote on October 12th,
1833 to his sister, referring to 'une simple et délicieuse
bourgeoise' (in all probability a young married woman of
twenty-four, Maria du Fresnay)[1] who, thanks to him, was
about to become a mother, and whose total self-surrender is
conveyed in the words, 'Aime-moi un an! Je t'aimerai toute
ma vie.' The same letter refers also to a more exigent
mistress, 'voluptueuse comme mille chattes'; she remains
unidentified. In August 1832 he had even tried to seduce
Zulma Carraud. Although she was not far from being in
love with him, we are entitled, knowing her sterling
character, to assume that loyalty to her husband was a
stronger motive for resistance than the realization that, at
that particular moment, any woman would have satisfied
him. Then had come the Castries humiliation which, if we
are to believe him, left a void in his heart.

Throughout his correspondence with his sister and Zulma
Carraud, it is plain that Balzac had been continually in
quest of a permanent and satisfying love. Hitherto all his
known affairs had been with women older than himself.
Mme de Berny in particular had responded to his craving
for the maternal affection of which, in his less grateful
moments, he felt he had been deprived. His infatuation for
L'Étrangère was no doubt in part an attempt to escape from
the attraction of older women. 'A trente-quatre ans . . . j'ai
déjà quelques cheveux blancs, et blanchir déjà sans avoir
été aimé par une jeune et jolie femme, cela est triste', he
writes to her in March 1833.[2] Perhaps even so a psycho-

---

[1] See A. Chancerel and R. Pierrot, 'La véritable Eugénie Grandet', in
Rev. des Sciences humaines, Oct.–Dec. 1955. In the autumn of 1833
Balzac was writing *Eugénie Grandet*, and the verbal portrait he paints
of his heroine is that of Maria to whom he dedicated the novel in 1839.
The child, born in June 1834, was a daughter, Marie, to whom Balzac
bequeathed Bouchardon's wood-carving of Christ in his will of 1847.

[2] *E.*, i, 16.

analyst would detect the persistence of the mother-wish in his letter of October 1833: 'Mon Dieu, que douce eût été cette journée où j'aurais pu jouer en liberté avec toi, comme un enfant joue avec sa mère!'[1] Such unsatisfied longings, and the salve for his hurt vanity which a liaison with a rich and nobly-born lady could provide, urged him to the expression of an idealized sentiment which only half-concealed more imperious, more erotic desires.

A meeting soon became possible. The Hanskis arrived in Switzerland for a holiday, in company with the Swiss nurse of their daughter Anna, Henriette Borel, who for many years acted as a go-between for their exchange of letters. In the last week of September 1833, at Neuchâtel, they took stock of each other for the first time, under the restraining eye of M. Hanski. Evelina probably had something of a shock at the sight of this rotund little bourgeois, gorgeously apparelled, but lacking the refinements and the artificialities of her class. But she was soon won over by his vitality and charm. He for his part was enchanted to find that the lady was personable as well as gracious. 'L'essentiel', he wrote to his sister, 'est que nous avons 27 ans [she had deceived him on this score], que nous sommes belle par admiration, que nous possédons les plus beaux cheveux noirs du monde, la peau suave et délicieusement fine des brunes, que nous avons une petite main d'amour, un cœur de 27 ans, naïf . . . imprudente au point de se jeter à mon cou devant tout le monde.'[2]

Ève did not throw herself at his neck, but they snatched one kiss. Then Balzac went home to rejoice in his *bonne fortune*, leaving Ève to hesitate between the impulse to sever all ties and rejoin him and religious scruples which urged her to pour her troubles into a confessor's ears. Neither of

[1] *E.*, i, 53.   [2] *L. F.*, 154.

these courses would have suited Balzac, and he dissuaded her, while pressing for a new meeting. When the Hanskis moved to Geneva, Balzac spent seven weeks there, from December 1833 to February 1834, in close proximity to them. This time the husband's surveillance was relaxed, and they became lovers. They exchanged tokens as well, and, with more enthusiasm than delicacy, adopted as their device the sacramental phrase 'adoremus in aeternum'. Already, at Neuchâtel, they had arrived at an understanding that they should be united when Ève became free. Hanski was twenty-two years older than Ève, and not robust. So was inaugurated a sometimes ecstatic, but more often tortured relationship which was regularized in marriage only after seventeen years; tortured not only because the 'chère épouse', as he now called her, was subject to periodic misgivings—moral and social scruples—but also because, in her more passionate moments, and these were plentiful, she could be jealous and viciously unkind. This jealousy was to be a torment for Balzac throughout the whole period of their relationship.

It extended to any woman with whom Balzac had social or friendly contacts. At Geneva already she was jealous of her own cousin, Countess Marie Potocka, a member of the Polish colony of exiles domiciled there, and with whom Balzac liked to converse. In Paris, she was jealous even of Mme Récamier, and more so still of Delphine de Girardin. Balzac had to be continually refuting her accusations, repeating that Ève was the only woman in his life save Mme de Berny, whose motherliness he over-emphasized as a means of diverting Ève from other and better-grounded suspicions. And he found it necessary to exaggerate the hermit-like seclusion in which he worked at the Rue Cassini as a proof of his constancy. She was jealous also of Mme de Castries, and not without cause, for when the latter came back from Italy in the summer of 1833, she made no scruple about resuming friendly relations with Balzac. On his return from Neuchâtel, he evidently wrote her a cruelly reproachful letter, and her reply suggests that it was Balzac who had been in the wrong for pressing too far 'un cœur qui vous donnait tout ce qu'il a encore d'affectueux'. Balzac repented of his harshness, and the spring of 1834 found him again on visiting terms with Henriette.

v. 'Lion', 'dandy'—and galley-slave

During this period of political ambition and emotional turmoil, Balzac's attempt to conquer Parisian society was perforce accompanied by a great increase in his personal and household expenses. Stimulated by the example of ostentation, passing for elegance, set him by such journalist associates as Eugène Sue, Jules Janin and Lautour-Mézeray, Balzac had begun to indulge in extravagance of dress, and in autumn 1831 had bought a cabriolet, a tilbury—as indispensable then as an expensive sports-model is to-day to a young blood—and two horses. He added to the number of rooms in his flat in the Rue Cassini, hired a coach-house and stable, and engaged a groom for whom he ordered a livery from his own tailor. This was Buisson, a life-long creditor whom Balzac had begun to patronize in his printing-house days, whom he occasionally advertised in his writings, and whom he had as a friend for many years. He it was who had supplied him with his blue coat with gold buttons, his numerous silk waistcoats of varying colours, his silk breeches and stockings, and his silver-buckled shoes. Balzac now had his flat redecorated, and furnished it with sumptuous carpets, silk hangings with lace embroideries, and a profusion of curtains. Being very much of a bibliophile, he enriched his library with expensive books and bindings.

Most men of artistic temperament crave for and need such material accessories to good living, and the only criticisms that one can make of Balzac's new mode of life are that his taste was far from impeccable, that his predominantly plebeian physique did not lend itself to adornment, and, more simply still, that he could not afford it. In the first five months of 1832, which was the year of a severe outbreak of cholera in Paris, he led a busy social life. His favourite resorts were still the salons of Baron Gérard, the Gays and Delphine de Girardin. He occasionally visited the salon of Mme O'Reilly, wife of one of the founders of *Le Temps*. There apparently he improved his acquaintance with the painter, Delacroix, whom he must have met casually on previous occasions. He also found himself drawn to opera, though it was probably not until 1834 that he actually subscribed for a seat in the notorious 'loge infernale' at the Opera-House: so-called because it was reputedly occupied by the 'tigres d'Opéra', the noisiest dandies of the capital. He was accused of giving more attention to the audience than to the performers; but it was there, or at that other home of musical drama, the Théâtre des Italiens, and also at public and private concerts that his education in music now began. It was developed further through the friendship of such musicians as Rossini, Berlioz and, from about 1833, Liszt; and, a little later still, Chopin. But it needed the Italian journeys of 1836–7, and the instruction of the eccentric composer, Jacques Strunz, the original of Schmucke in *Le cousin Pons*, for him to obtain enough technical knowledge for the writing of *Gambara* and *Massimila Doni*. Although he himself was too clumsy to dance, he also went to Opera balls, one of which he later described in the first part of *Splendeurs et misères des courtisanes*. He continued to be a familiar figure at fashionable cafés and eating-houses.

Hospitality which he received in the country, from Mme de Berny, the Margonnes and the Carrauds, helped him to cut down expenditure, but by July 1832 he was in such straits that, from Angoulême, he instructed his mother, whom he had left in charge of his affairs at the Rue Cassini, to sell his cabriolet and other trappings of his dandyism. Then an opportune loan from Mme Delannoy tided over his embarrassments and permitted the further excursion to Aix and Geneva with Mme de Castries. And there was no real halt in his career of extravagance.

By 1833 Balzac had attained at least one of his ambitions and become a veritable 'lion' of the salons. His fame was spreading in Germany, and in France he won admiration from women-readers especially: they were grateful for the understanding his stories showed of their needs and aspirations. He found his presence demanded, not only by Mme Récamier, Delphine de Girardin and the Comtesse d'Agoult,[1] the future mistress of Liszt who became a novelist under the pen-name of Daniel Stern, but by ladies of more exalted rank, tired of sulking with their class over the change of monarch, such as the Duchesse de Rauzun, who had the most brilliant salon of the Faubourg Saint-Germain, and the Marquise de la Bourdonnaye. His ardent and genial personality and his magical gifts as a raconteur gave him real entertainment value, and he was regarded as a social acquisition, except by the snobs whom his sartorial and conversational indiscretions annoyed. Rodolphe Apponyi gives in his memoirs an account of an evening in the salon of Mme de la Bourdonnaye in March 1833, and takes a malicious

---

[1] So says L. J. Arrigon (*Les Années romantiques de Balzac*, 1927, p. 255), probably on the authority of Count Rodolphe Apponyi's *Journal* (1913–26), ii, 368–70. But Balzac wrote to George Sand on 18 January 1840 that he had not met Mme d'Agoult. See, in *Revue des Études Hongroises*, Jan.–June 1934, Th. Marix's 'Histoire d'une amitié: Fr. Liszt et H. de Balzac' (pp. 42–3).

pleasure in relating how Balzac was embarrassed, and then infuriated, by the running comments of his rival and enemy, Jules Janin, while he told a fantastic story of love on a desert island. From such mortifications the kind and witty Delphine de Girardin must have protected him in her salon. In return Balzac gave her hints on novel-writing, called her his 'écolière', frequently visited her and went out with her, all the while minimizing the cordiality of his friendship with her for the benefit of Ève. 'L'Étrangère', quite without reason, suspected the pair of closer ties. Delphine was a delightful hostess and friend to all the great writers of Paris, but to none more than to Balzac. Throughout the years of his vexed and fitful relations with Émile de Girardin as a newspaper-proprietor, she spared no effort to keep the peace between her hard-bitten husband and the necessitous, irascible man of genius.

To maintain this pace of life, to pay the bills of tailors, jewellers, furnishers and caterers, and also to find the money for his travels abroad, he needed much money; and his earning of it always fell behind the spending of it. In consequence the debt which had subsisted from 1828 swelled from year to year. He got into the habit of selling works not yet written, and sometimes never to be written. He received and spent advance payments for them, which he had to return with interest and indemnities when he failed to produce his copy. He incurred new obligations before the old ones were cleared off, and so accumulated mortgages on his time and energy which, besides keeping him in trouble with editors and publishers, confirmed him in that way of life for which he became famous: orgies of work punctuated by orgies of relaxation and pleasure, one necessitating the other —a vicious circle from which in the end only disease and death released him. He himself in his letters, and friends and associates in their reminiscences[1] have expatiated on the theme of the long periods that he spent at his writing-table, clad in his white quasi-monastic robe, wielding his raven's quill-pen, chasing fatigue and seeking inspiration by means of that poisonously strong black coffee which, coupled with his lack of exercise and fresh air, eventually undermined his health.

It was in these early years that he settled down to a programme of work that would soon have brought an ordinary man to mental breakdown: dinner at 6 p.m., bed till 1 a.m., work till 8 a.m., rest till 9.30, then a cup of coffee, and work again till 4 p.m. Then the reception of visitors, a bath or an excursion out of doors; then dinner and bed; and so on for weeks and fortnights. Thus he described his manner of life in 1833 to Zulma Carraud.[2] This programme was subject to variation, but in principle it remained the same. As the pressure of inspiration—or commitments—increased, so did his hours of work, from fourteen to sixteen, and sometimes to eighteen hours a day. Even his method of composition added to his embarrassments. His process of creation was an exceptional one. Many of his works he seems to have carried in his head before setting a word down on paper. They were so real to him that he regarded them as already finished, and he was probably not being consciously dishonest when he declared that such and such a novel was written, and sold it as such. 'Je l'ai là,' he said, tapping his forehead, of an unwritten article of 1836, 'Je n'ai plus qu'à l'écrire'.[3] But once he had mapped out a scheme or drafted out a story in manuscript, his habit was to have a first proof printed. He then, by dint of marginal insertions and corrections which

---

[1] Gozlan, in *Balzac en pantoufles* (1856) and *Balzac chez lui* (1862); Werdet in *Portrait intime* (1859); Gautier in *Portraits contemporains* (1858–74).

[2] Z. C., 118.   [3] Werdet, *Portrait intime*, 225.

made the proof well-nigh undecipherable (an hour of Balzac was enough for the ordinary compositor), revised, added, altered, re-wrote and expanded. This process was repeated time and time again. He reached a record with *Pierrette* (1839–40), for which he had twenty-nine proofs.[1] Printers and publishers were reduced to despair; when in the end the book came out he had considerably diminished his own receipts by the amount of the proof bills which all of his publishers, once they had got used to his ways, stipulated that he should pay.

The story of Balzac's dealings with his publishers is so repetitive as to become wearisome. He had quarrelled with Latouche in 1829 over the loss that the latter had incurred in connection with *Le dernier Chouan*. He tired out his publishers, or grew tired of them, one by one: after Urbain Canel it was Gosselin, after Gosselin Mame, after Mame Mme Béchet, after Mme Béchet Werdet, who in a couple of years was reduced to bankruptcy. And so on throughout the years. To follow out the references to them in his correspondence is to note how invariably affectionate epithets change to abusive ones. Gosselin ends up as a 'rost-beef ambulant', and Mame as an 'ignoble bourreau . . . gibier de bagne . . . scorpion humain'. It fell to Werdet, in his *Portrait intime*, to pay him back in his own coin, and to exclaim against his pride, boastfulness, lust for wealth and other short-comings; also, in *Souvenirs de la vie littéraire* of 1879, to quote the remark of an unnamed writer: 'Les éditeurs sont faits pour être *ruinés* par des hommes tels que Balzac.'

Not only did he rarely fulfil his contracts in time, but once or twice he contracted for the same projected work with different publishers.[2] His dealings with newspaper editors

[1] According to an article by M. Bouteron, in *La Presse*, 9 Feb. 1928.
[2] e.g. the unwritten *Bataille* in 1831 (Mame, Boulland, Dieulouard). See M. Bouteron: *Cahiers balzaciens*, No. I, p. xii.

followed the same trend. He quarrelled with them over the price he should receive for his contributions, or because his works were not favourably reviewed in the periodicals for which he was writing, or because—this was the worst offence—they occasionally printed a contribution before he had made his final corrections and given his 'bon à tirer'. Such artistic scrupulousness was laudable, although it was accompanied by that touchiness and pride which are not uncommon with men of letters. But his troubles were normally caused by his impatience to make money. He was shrewd and business-like in making his contracts, but either too burdened with work or too intent upon perfection to fulfil them with sufficient promptitude.

And so Balzac found himself chained to the treadmill which he went on working for the rest of his life. It is tempting to suppose that, his nature being what it was, in no other conditions could he have been brought to accomplish the vast purpose which, round about 1833, was taking shape in his imagination. Was the goad of ever-mounting debt needed to make him press forward? Can we even speak of a general conspiracy of circumstances which closed other avenues and issues and turned Balzac into what he was plainly intended to be, a kind of battery-hen for the laying of that formidable clutch of literary eggs known as the 'Human Comedy'? To suggest so much would be to ignore an essential fact: the sense of genius, the creative urge within him, the knowledge that a whole world was stirring just below the surface of his consciousness and that his vocation was to bring it forth. The demonic joy which his power to do so gave him more than compensated for his Cyclopean labours.

Here was the real driving-force. Nevertheless, the collapse of marriage schemes, the frustration of political hopes, the mortification of the Castries affair which was, in a way, a symbol of his failure to impose himself upon the legitimist party, the popularity of his scenes and tales, the persuasion that they could be used for expressing the turmoil of ideas and convictions that welled up inside him: all these factors combined with material embarrassments to make him the victim of his own phenomenal productivity. But this slave to a purpose had his twists and turns, his evasions and flights —at the end of a not too long tether which always pulled him back again. They make the rest of his life a confused, entertaining and yet pathetic picture.

III

TUMULTUOUS YEARS, 1834–41

*Il y a quelque chose de plus comique
que Molière; c'est l'intérêt personnel.*
Letter to Mme Hanska

i. From the Rue Cassini to the Rue des Batailles. 1834–5

IN 1833 Mme Béchet had established herself as Balzac's most favoured publisher. In December of that year she brought out the first two volumes of the 'Études de Mœurs'. In due course his unpunctuality wore out her patience and his relations with her became cool. Her successor was near at hand: her own managing clerk, Edmond Werdet, who was thrown much in Balzac's way and conceived a great admiration for him. He had himself been a publisher, though unsuccessful, before he worked for Mme Béchet. He was energetic, ambitious and persuasive. No doubt Balzac borrowed some traits from him for the glib and enterprising travelling salesman, *L'illustre Gaudissart*.[1] It was not long before Werdet thought of setting up on his own again with the hope of superseding Balzac's other publishers. His first overtures were rebuffed, but he persevered, and Balzac sold him the right to publish a new edition of *Le Médecin de campagne*. Other contracts ensued, and his appetite was whetted. He began publication of the 'Études Philosophiques' in January 1835, and Balzac agreed that, by buying out other publishers as time went on, he should become to him what Constable had been to Scott. The prospect was dazzling but full of danger.

[1] *E.* i, 173, 15 July 1834: 'L'illustre Werdet, qui ressemble un peu à *L'Illustre Gaudissart*. . . .' This story was written in 1833. Balzac first alludes to Werdet in a letter to Mme Hanska of 24 October 1833. (*E.*, i, 62.)

A notable expansion of Balzac's social relationships occurred in 1834. Before he left Geneva Marie Potocka gave
him a letter of introduction to Countess Apponyi, wife of
the Austrian ambassador in Paris. From the end of February he became a regular visitor to her salon: a matter for
great satisfaction, for the Apponyis received most exalted
guests from court and aristocratic circles. He was able to
gain attention at these gatherings. On May 7th, for instance,
he was holding forth on two of his pet subjects, magnetism
and thought-transference, to that distinguished diplomat,
the Duc de Laval. Moreover, his reception there gained him
admission into other ambassadorial circles, as, for example, in
1835, the salon of Mme Kisseleff, wife of the Russian
chargé d'affaires. He was soon to meet Prince Esterhazy
and receive flattering attentions from Prince Schönburg.

His self-esteem as a dandy and 'viveur' was much en-
hanced. He had given up using his tilbury, and so he hired
a coupé by the month, with his coat of arms blazoned on its
panels. Not content with vivid waistcoats, he took to a
lorgnette, and, in August 1834, began to astonish and amuse
Paris by parading the most famous of his walking-sticks,
made for him by the jeweller Lecointe at a cost of 700
francs. 'La Canne de M. de Balzac' was large and ornate.
The knob was of gold, and studded with turquoises. The
hinged cap concealed a small box in which, later, he kept a
miniature of Mme Hanska; attached to the stick was a gold
chain which she had worn round her neck as a child. This
stick, promptly seized upon by such caricaturists as Dantan,
is a symbol both of his social vanity and his childish love of
baubles. But it was good for publicity, and he knew it. 'J'ai
créé la secte des "Cannophiles" dans le monde élégant,' he
boasted to Ève, 'et l'on me prend pour un homme frivole.
Cela m'amuse.' Elsewhere he related how, one evening at

the Opera, a young elegant begged the honour of having his own stick formally presented to the novelist's resplendent toy.

He was still spending money on his rue Cassini flat, buying bronzes, silver plate, household ornaments, and more furniture and carpets. One of the novel features in this flat was the secret door which, so hints Werdet, enabled clandestine visitors to slip away discreetly from his sumptuously furnished bedroom. For the purchase of knick-knacks he excused himself to Ève on the grounds that, like his visits to operas and concerts, they were his sole distractions. But he enjoyed many others besides. He sometimes offered royal entertainment to his fast-living friends—the satellites of Olympe Pélissier and the fellow-dandies with whom he consorted at the Opera. Dinners at the Rocher de Cancale and similar resorts of epicures were no doubt a necessary part of the game he was playing. In April 1834 he was present at a different kind of dinner, one which he must have found more interesting still. It was given by the philanthropist Benjamin Appert, with the retired executioner Sanson and the notorious Vidocq, ex-convict and former chief of security police,[1] as fellow-guests. When he relaxed from work, he recouped himself for the rigours of asceticism by such gargantuan repasts as that described in *Portrait intime*, a private orgy at Véry's restaurant. Werdet gaped with stupefaction while Balzac addressed himself to a hundred oysters, twelve lamb cutlets, a duck, a brace of partridges, a 'sole meunière', with full accompaniments of hors d'œuvres, sweets, fruit and vintage wines. Even allowing for Werdet's habitual ex-

[1] See M. Bouteron, 'En marge du Père Goriot: Balzac, Vidocq et Sanson', in *La Revue*, 1 Jan. 1948, and P. Vernière, 'Balzac et la genèse de Vautrin', in *R.H.L.F.*, Jan.–March 1948. J. Savant, in *Les vrais Mémoires de Vidocq*, 1950, states that B. had first met Vidocq in 1822 and had since drawn much literary inspiration from his confidences. Later relations between B. and V. are enlarged upon by Gozlan in *B. chez lui*.

aggeration, it must have been a memorable meal. Gastritis prevented Werdet from sharing in this feast, but the cost of it went to swell his private account with Balzac. He found it impossible to resist the fascination of Balzac's eccentricities, and was foolishly easy-going in advancing money and endorsing his bills. Creditors swarmed, but Balzac was so confident of his ability to wipe out his debts by his pen that he seems by now to have given up all idea of respectable bourgeois solvency.

He was working hard. He drove himself, and was ready to drive other people. In the autumn of 1834 Jules Sandeau came to live with him at the rue Cassini. Balzac was sorry for George Sand's ex-lover, but his hospitality was not disinterested. He expected a *quid pro quo* from his guest, as later from other down-at-heel writers like Charles Lassailly: proof correction, aid with correspondence, collaboration in ideas for plays, and patience in listening to readings and discussions of his works. It was in this same autumn that he sent to Mme Hanska the famous letter[1] outlining the now clearly-conceived plan for the three-fold organization of his writings as 'Études de Moeurs', 'Études philosophiques' and 'Études analytiques', the first representing the 'social effects' whose 'causes' should be studied in the second, the third representing the 'principles' lying at the base of social life. At the turn of the year 1834–5, even while that greatest of novels, *Le Père Goriot*, was appearing in the *Revue de Paris*, he was entrusting to a friend from *Figaro* days, Félix Davin, the task of explaining his ultimate purpose in Introductions to the collected *Scènes de la vie privée* and the 'Études philosophiques' which Mme Béchet and Werdet respectively were about to publish. By this means the *Scènes* were at last methodically classified and the logic of their succession un-

[1] *E.* i, 205; 20 Oct. 1834.

folded, with the intention that the scenes of private, provincial, Parisian, political, military and country life, besides presenting 'l'histoire sociale faite dans toutes ses parties,' should tell the story of individual human experience from adolescence to old age. Not even the *Avant-Propos* of the 'Comédie Humaine', which Balzac gave to the world seven years later, was to reveal in such detail the end for which he was now consciously striving in spite of distractions and persecutions.

Creditors were not the only persecutors he had to face— or to evade. The Monarchy of July had renewed the 'citizen-army' of the National Guard, and all able citizens were required by law to take their turn in parades and guard-duty. The penalty for default was detention in the Hotel Bazan-court, a building set aside for this purpose, and generally known as the 'Hotel des Haricots'. In 1835 Balzac was thrice condemned for failure to attend his drills, and although he avoided incarceration this year by evasion or bribery, he was finding himself too much sought-after in the rue Cassini for life to be tranquil. And so, in March, leaving Sandeau at the flat, for the lease had still some time to run, he rented a set of rooms out at Chaillot, at No. 13 rue des Batailles, under the name of Mme Veuve Durand. As a further precaution against disturbance, he arranged that his letters should be addressed to his valet Auguste Depril, whose name he ennobled to 'de Pril', and adopted a system of pass-words to be used by his friends.

Au portier l'on disait, 'La saison des prunes est arrivée', et il vous laissait franchir le seuil; au domestique accouru sur l'escalier au son de la cloche, il fallait murmurer, 'J'apporte des dentelles de Belgique', et si vous assuriez au valet de chambre que 'madame Bertrand était en bonne santé', on vous introduisait enfin.[1]

[1] Th. Gautier: *H. de Balzac*, 1858; article of 1858 (in *l'Artiste*) collected in *Portraits contemporains* (1874); reprinted in *Souvenirs Romantiques* (Garnier, 1929), p. 139.

This seclusion, though far less complete than he would have had Mme Hanska believe, gave 'Mme Veuve Durand' a good opportunity for further hard work, which was to bear fruit in the completion of the mystical *Séraphita* and the composition of those curiously contrasting novels, the sardonically realist *Contrat de mariage* (*La Fleur-des-Pois*) and the sentimental *Lys dans la vallée*. But seclusion and discomfort are not synonymous. Once installed, he began to improve his quarters. The new flat was famed for the oriental richness of the salon, with its colour-scheme of black and white, pink and gold, its massive Turkish divan, its red hangings, taffeta-lined muslin curtains, and Persian carpet. We owe the description of it to Balzac himself, as given in *La Fille aux yeux d'or*, which he was finishing early in 1835. For this story of Lesbian passion ending in bloody tragedy he needed a setting which should have all the voluptuousness of an Eastern harem. And so the boudoir in which the unhappy Paquita Valdès is kept a prisoner by the jealous and possessive Marquise de San Real is an exact replica of the Chaillot salon.

So Théophile Gautier affirms. But since the composition of the narrative and the decoration of the flat took place almost simultaneously, it is equally possible that the salon was an attempt to translate the fictitious boudoir into real fact. The boudoir was so constructed that nothing that went on inside could be heard from outside: 'cette retraite a été construite pour l'amour,' says Paquita to Henri de Marsay, 'aucun son ne s'en échappe.' Balzac went on to pad the salon until it too was virtually sound-proof. Gautier smilingly rules out the suggestion that the salon was intended to serve a similar purpose to that of the boudoir.

ii. Between three loves. 1834–5

Balzac looked back on the Geneva meeting as 'une des plus douces haltes que j'aie faites dans ma vie de fantassin littéraire'. After this happy interlude his letters followed Ève on her journeys through Northern Italy to Vienna, where she and her husband made a prolonged stay. Once she expressed fears of pregnancy, and Balzac speculated over the exceptional qualities which the son of such a mother—and such a father—might hope to possess. He had much to write about. He gave her news of the ailing Mme de Berny, recounted his negotiations with publishers and the progress of his work, and had much ado in allaying her suspicions about Henriette de Castries. In mid-February 1834[1] he was urging, as an excuse for visiting the latter, the necessity of submitting *La Duchesse de Langeais* to her, to win her approval of what he had written about the Faubourg Saint-Germain.[2] Three weeks later he told Ève: 'me voilà, à cause de *La Duchesse de Langeais*, brouillé avec Mme de C. . . .'[3] There is no other evidence that Henriette resented this novel as an act of vengeance against her: and yet she surely must have recognized it as being such, at least in part, however much the fiction may alter and disguise the real event which gave it birth.[4]

The embroilment with Henriette of which Balzac here speaks only became serious in the autumn: on the 18th October he wrote her a cold and formal letter which makes it clear that he had a new grievance against her. Its apparent cause was the bitter undertone of her eulogy of the recently-published *Recherche de l'absolu*. Its real cause was jealousy:

[1] *E.*, i, 131.   [2] See above, p. 52.   [3] *E.*, i, 138.
[4] See in *Revue d'Histoire littéraire*, Oct.–Dec. 1947, the article by G. Thouvenin, 'La composition de "La Duchesse de Langeais",' which shows how Balzac utilized a love affair of the poet Ulric Guttinguer for the plot of the novel.

Henriette had just read *Volupté*, Sainte-Beuve's story of platonic love, had written an admiring letter to its author, and was laying the foundations of a sentimental friendship with him. To the impertinence of thus capturing Henriette's attention Sainte-Beuve added the further one of disparaging him in a November issue of the *Revue des deux Mondes*, and Balzac decided to avenge himself by 're-writing *Volupté*': 'Je lui passerai ma plume au travers du corps'. *Le Lys dans la vallée* was the outcome of this resolution.

In the meantime, Henriette gave lively expression to the pain which his October letter had caused her, but this new breach between them was soon healed. It was possibly about this time, however, that she played a malicious trick on him. In order to see how far his author's vanity would take him, she persuaded an Irish governess living in Paris, Miss Margaret Patrickson, to write him love-letters purporting to come from a 'Lady Nevil'. He fell into the trap, and responded in kind. After receiving three letters from him, Miss Patrickson was stricken with remorse, disclosed her true identity, and appears to have won his benevolence by so doing. Only in June 1837 did she tell him that Henriette had been the prime mover in this little plot.[1] Had he known this in 1834 he might have severed with Henriette alto-gether. As it was, their relations became markedly tender again in 1835, when he was making epistolary love to her and Ève simultaneously. He gave her Christian name to Mme de Mortsauf, the heroine of *Le Lys dans la vallée*, and remained on affectionate terms with her, at any rate until 1836. He continued to visit her in Paris, and sometimes at the country houses of her father, the Duc de Maillé, and her

[1] For a summary of Balzac's relationship with Miss Patrickson, see S. R. B. Smith, *B. et l'Angleterre* (London, 1953; privately printed by Williams, Lee & Co.), pp. 35–6. Her letters, communicated by M. Bouteron, are reproduced pp. 178–83.

uncle Fitz-James. But all the time he felt himself forced to exaggerate to Ève the effects of Henriette's spinal malady, representing it not only as diminishing her attractions but also as threatening her life.

His love-letters to Ève, clandestinely collected by Ève or Henriette Borel, alternated with formal missives which were fit for a husband's perusal. When in the summer of 1834 two of the love-letters fell into M. Hanski's hands he had to pass them off as mere exercises written to show Mme Hanska how Alphonse de Montauran, the hero of *Les Chouans*, might have written to the heroine, Marie de Verneuil. The storm blew over, and M. Hanski became affable again. No doubt he felt flattered to be on familiar terms with a great French writer, whose attentions to his wife, moreover, kept her in an amiable frame of mind. Also he was, like his wife, interested in autographs, and Balzac kept them supplied with these. In May 1836 he presented Balzac with a malachite inkstand. Later, in 1837, after Louis Boulanger had painted his famous portrait of Balzac, the original of which went to Wierzchownia, M. Hanski footed the bill.

After this mishap Balzac went more warily. In February 1834 he had been fatuously direct: 'Vois-tu; l'amour d'un poète tient un peu de la folie. Il n'y a que les artistes qui soient dignes des femmes, parce qu'ils sont un peu femmes.'[1] After October of that year he was more often content with oblique protestations of attachment: 'l'inconstance, l'infidélité sont des *incompréhensibilités* pour moi. Rien ne me lasse, ni l'attente, ni le bonheur. Mon amitié est de la race des granits. . . .' A letter of 26th November, 1834 shows him flattering Ève for her 'immense superiority of mind'. But all the time he had been looking forward to a new meeting.

[1] *E.*, i, 126.

This at last became possible in May 1835, with the aid of a loan from Werdet.

On the 9th May he set out from Paris in a hired barouche, with his valet resplendent in a new livery. He himself was equipped with brand-new trunks stamped with the pseudo-d'Entragues arms. 'M. le Marquis de Balzac', as a Viennese admirer, Countess Loulou Thurheim, facetiously styled him, arrived at Vienna on the 16th. He settled down at the Hotel de la Poire for nineteen days, and divided his time between working at *Le Lys dans la vallée*, social calls, and visits to the Hanski domicile. He was well received in fashionable circles, made friends with the aged Metternich and the latter's third wife, Princess Mélanie; was taken by Prince Friedrich Schwarzenberg to survey the battlefield of Wagram with a view to a 'scene from military life' which he was hoping to write; and he received a flattering ovation one evening at a public concert. Furthermore, a meeting with the distinguished orientalist, Baron von Hammer-Purgstall, who had translated into Arabic for him the inscription on the talisman of *La Peau de chagrin*, resulted in Balzac's acquisition of his famous lucky charm, the stone mounted in a ring and bearing the magic word BEDOUCK in Arabic characters. His superstitious mind made much of this gewgaw—for some months at any rate. To-day in France many of the Balzacian specialists jestingly use the mystic word 'bedouck' as a form of salutation.

The course of love did not run altogether smoothly at Vienna. The proximity of a husband, however myopic or easy-going, may have caused both the lovers some nervous tension, and some of the hours they spent together were more tantalizing than satisfying.[1] There were sharp ex-

[1] *E.*, i, 254. . . . 'je n'ai jamais été si heureux, je n'ai jamais tant souffert. Un cœur plus ardent que l'imagination n'est vive est un funeste présent, quand le bonheur complet n'étanche pas la soif de tous les jours.'

changes and stormy scenes, which were to leave a deep impression on Balzac. On his way back from Vienna he paused at Munich to call on that notorious Englishwoman Jane Digby, Lady Ellenborough, now living with a new husband, Baron Venningen, and soon to move further east until by stages her quest for the perfect love brought her to the harem of an Arab sheikh. Balzac had obviously met her before, doubtless in 1830 or 1831, when she was living in Paris with Prince Felix Schwarzenberg. An unauthenticated tradition asserts that he had even enjoyed her favours at that time.[1] What is certain, for he himself admitted it to Ève in 1840,[2] is that the Munich visit gave him some ideas for the character of the ardently voluptuous Lady Arabella Dudley, the rival of Mme de Mortsauf in *Le Lys dans la vallée*. But by now another Englishwoman had swum into the ken of this inconsistent Anglophobe.

The incidents in Balzac's sentimental life so far recorded have made it fairly clear that he was incapable of uninterrupted fidelity. It is true that he made frequent professions of continence. Both early and late in his career he expressed the conviction that dalliance with women, besides wasting time, saps creative energy. He even endowed his working garment, the quasi-monastic habit, with symbolic meaning: 'La robe blanche exprime la sobriété, la continence, la pureté qui prolongent la vie et entretiennent les forces toujours actives, toujours vertes.'[3] Gautier tells us that the only concession he made to authors was that they might spend a half-hour with their beloved once a year and write them letters: 'cela formait le style.'[4] Love-letters did more

---

[1] See E. M. Oddie, *Portrait of Ianthe* (1935) and Lesley Branch, *The Wilder Shores of Love* (1954).
[2] *E.*, i, 538, 15 May, 1840.
[3] *Les Martyrs ignorés*, Conard, *O. D.*, iii, 136.
[4] *Op cit.*, in *Souvenirs Romantiques*, 127.

than that for Balzac—they enabled him to keep his writer's imagination in the desired state of excitation. But in spite of these dogmatic utterances, he could not live indefinitely on day-dreams, platonic effusions and protracted hopes. After Vienna the Hanskis went back to Wierzchownia, and the prospect of a new meeting within a measurable space of time became slender. A substitute for the inaccessible *princesse lointaine* was already close at hand. In the early summer of 1834, at the Apponyis', Balzac had met Sarah Frances Lowell.

This beautiful Englishwoman with ash-blond hair was the wife of an Italian nobleman, Count Guidoboni-Visconti, a man of illustrious birth but diminished fortune, delicate in health, and given to eccentric hobbies—playing the violin in theatre orchestras, and washing and labelling medicine-bottles for chemists. The couple lived in Paris, but had a summer residence at Versailles. The Countess, if we are to believe the malevolent Lambinet, belonged to an undisciplined family and had not an irreproachable past. That she and Balzac were soon friendly is proved by the fact that, in October 1834 and after, he shared with her and her husband a box at the Théâtre des Italiens. To Zulma Carraud on 17th April 1835, he writes that he is 'depuis quelques jours sous la domination d'une personne fort envahissante'. This might be Sarah, to whom Balzac is still apparently referring, four years later, as 'la diva'. After his return from Vienna the friendship seems to have ripened quickly. There is no solid proof that she and Balzac were lovers, but there is documentary evidence that he made two journeys to Boulogne-sur-Mer in June and August 1835. From that it has been deduced that he was accompanying Sarah on her way to England, and even that they may have crossed the Channel together. According to Lambinet she had already had a son by the profligate Prince Koslovsky, whose daughter, Sophie, was a close friend of hers. At the end of May 1836 she gave birth to a second son, Lionel Richard, and Balzac is reputed to have been his father. The first of these two baptismal names might well have given rise to a different theory, for in the summer of 1835, again by the testimony of Lambinet, the philanderer Lionel de Bonneval had been a dangerous competitor for Sarah's affections.

Gossip and conjecture: upon this foundation rests the view that the relationship between Balzac and Sarah was a tender one for several years. And yet it is difficult to deny that the probabilities favour this view.[1] In any case she was a staunch friend, helpful and generous. Conjecture again has credited her with having influenced certain of Balzac's works: *Séraphita, Le Secret des Ruggieri*,[2] *L'Enfant maudit*[3] and *Mémoires de deux jeunes mariées*.[4] It has also been thought that, besides providing a second model for Arabella Dudley in *Le Lys*, she lent some features to Fanny O'Brien, Baronne du Guénic, in *Béatrix*, a work which Balzac dedicated to 'Sarah'. Her repeated advances of money to Balzac, and the way she stood by him in certain crises, justifies Balzac's own portrait of her in 1840—'une des plus aimables femmes, et d'une infinie, d'une exquise bonté.'[5] Perhaps the ambiguity of this relationship, in which she seems to have played a patient and unselfish rôle, is best conveyed in a remark of Arabella to Félix de Vandenesse: 'Votre amie toujours, et votre maîtresse quand vous le voudrez.'

[1] Writing before *Balzac mis à nu* was published, Henry Prior rejected the supposition (in 'Balzac à Turin', *Revue de Paris*, 15 Jan. 1924).
[2] 1836–7; later to form Part II of *Sur Catherine de Médicis*.
[3] Begun in 1831, but not completed until 1836.
[4] First conceived 1834–5, expanded and developed 1840–1.
[5] *E.*, i, 530, 10 Feb. 1840.

iii. 'Une douloureuse année'. 1836

Whatever distraction Balzac may have derived from his friendship with Sarah, clouds were gathering on his horizon as 1835 drew to a close. His debts were increasing and he was now looking back on the Viennese excursion as a folly from the financial point of view. It was true that he was arranging with a new publisher, Hippolyte Souverain, for the publication of his collected *Œuvres de Jeunesse*, for which he was to receive 10,000 francs, while two needy but titled 'secrétaires'—the Count (later Marquis) de Belloy and Count Ferdinand de Gramont—were engaged to complete and prepare them for publication. But he sustained a considerable loss when, on December 12th, a fire which broke out at a printers' warehouse destroyed a large part of the third 'dizain' of the *Contes Drolatiques* and 250 copies of the first and second 'dizains'. Then also Balzac discovered that François Buloz, editor of the *Revue de Paris* in which *Le Lys dans la vallée* was beginning to appear, had sold the first part of the novel to the *Gazette Étrangère de St. Pétersbourg*, which had published it before it appeared in Paris and what is more, had taken the text from an uncorrected proof. Balzac was justifiably incensed, and a quarrel began which rapidly developed into a lawsuit—impudently started by Buloz himself. At the same time Balzac was so disgusted by the treatment meted out to him by Buloz' two reviews, the *Revue de Paris* and the *Revue des Deux Mondes*, and the press in general that he decided to run a periodical of his own. He bought up from one William Duckett a major share in the derelict *Chronique de Paris*.

During the first six months of 1836 therefore he had two important affairs on his hands, the lawsuit with Buloz and the business of running a periodical. He had paid little for his share in it, but incurred heavy liabilities for the maintenance of it. He appointed his friend Émile Regnault as 'gérant', and applied himself with gusto to the task of gathering a staff around him: Théophile Gautier, the Besançon novelist Charles de Bernard, the critic Gustave Planche, conveniently filched from the Buloz reviews, Alphonse Karr and others. Jules Sandeau was also included, but he gave up in March, being no longer able to stand the strain of collaboration with Balzac: he had lived on his hospitality for eighteen months. The *Chronique de Paris* appeared twice a week. It had political as well as literary significance, for Balzac was again intent on forming a party, that of the 'Intelligentiels', with the *Chronique* as its organ. He faced with relish the task of ruling an editorial staff and setting the world to rights, and for three months he worked strenuously, giving good fare to subscribers with his own stories,[1] his political and critical articles, the 'nouvelles' of Charles de Bernard and Gautier. This venture marks the beginning of a cordial and enduring friendship between Balzac and Gautier, who admired the genius of his senior and was amused by his personality. What he later wrote about Balzac, both as man and writer, is of great value.

Unfortunately there were not enough subscribers. By March Balzac was looking round for fresh capital. By June the review was moribund, and Balzac was taking a holiday at Saché to recover from the strain of anxiety and overwork. In July he accepted defeat and relinquished the *Chronique* with a new debt of 46,000 francs on his hands, part of which was owed to Duckett, who was to prove a merciless creditor. This venture had ended almost as disastrously as those of

[1] *La Messe de l'athée, L'Interdiction, Facino Cane,* 15 pages of *Le Cabinet des antiques.* Part ii of *L'Enfant maudit* and *Le Secret des Ruggieri* appeared in the *Chronique* towards the end of the year, but by then the periodical was no longer his.

1826–8, and probably for the same reason—Balzac's incapacity for business management.

Balzac's career as editor had not been made easier by a week's incarceration in the 'Hotel des Haricots', which he suffered from the 27th of April to the 4th of May 1836. He still lived occasionally in his old flat in the Rue Cassini, and it was there that the officers of the National Guard caught him. A man of his buoyancy was not likely to sit down and bite his nails during such confinement. He called for help—and funds—from Werdet, and although the arrogance of Eugène Sue, who was arrested the same day, annoyed him, his captivity was sweetened by merry-making and dinner-parties, and women admirers sent him gifts and expressions of sympathy. When he came out the Buloz lawsuit was upon him. The case was heard on May 15th, but judgment was postponed. In the meantime the *Revue de Paris*, in an article of May 29th, did its best to prejudge the issue by telling the long tale of its grievances against Balzac. The latter retaliated by publishing in his own *Chronique* an 'Historique du Procès' which appeared also as a preface to the edition of *Le Lys* that Werdet was waiting to bring out as soon as the affair was over. It gave his side of the case, and enabled him to vent his spleen against some of Buloz' supporters. Judgment was delivered on June 3rd: it was a complete vindication for Balzac. He was awarded costs, but no damages. He had just cause for resentment at this, for Buloz' unscrupulousness had forced him to waste both time and money.

At the turn of the year he was to look back on it and call it 'une douloureuse année'. He was beset by other than legal, editorial and financial woes. The Hanskis were back in the Ukraine. Ève's probings and scoldings were almost continuous. Was he working as hard as he pretended? Was he paying too much attention to 'la princesse G . . .?' What was she to make of Aunt Rosalie's hints that he was married, or that he had taken to gambling? Aunt Rosalie was a busybody with a house in Vienna where scandal from Paris was received and canvassed. To appease Ève's inquisitiveness, Balzac wrote variations on the theme of 'le solitaire sur son rocher avec sa cruche et son pain'. Throughout the year he had cause to reproach her for her hardness and lack of understanding. We do not know how much consolation he was getting from Sarah during his *Chronique de Paris* troubles, but he derived at least spiritual comfort in the spring from a new source. Some time in March, while he was writing *Facino Cane* (which he dedicated to her in 1844), a mysterious lady of supposedly high rank wrote him another of those attractive anonymous letters which came his way so often. He replied, and a correspondence ensued which went on fairly regularly for months. The only facts one can surmise from Balzac's letters to her[1] are that her name was Louise, that her birthday was on August 25th, that she knew or professed to know her Faubourg Saint-Germain (she criticized Balzac's account of it in *La Duchesse de Langeais*), that she was married and had a child, and that she suffered a misfortune in August 1836.[2] She had artistic talent, and sent Balzac some products of her pencil and her brush. She also had sent him flowers while he was in the 'Hotel des Haricots'.

Perhaps in answering Louise's letters he was hoping to begin a romance which should have a happier dénouement than the one with Henriette de Castries. In fact her method of approach, so like that of Henriette, awoke in him the

[1] Collected in vol. xxiv of the *Ed. Déf.*, pp. 247–68.

[2] A note attached to the copy of her letters at Chantilly asserts that she was the wife of a somewhat obscure dramatist. One of her letters states that 'Louise' was not the Christian name she usually went by.

memory of what he had suffered at her hands. But the lady insisted on remaining anonymous, and no meeting ever came about. Balzac accepted the situation, with some show of chivalry, but also with some moments of irritation at being so frustrated. When she wrote 'Aimez-moi comme on aime Dieu', he replied 'Il n'y a que ceux qui voient Dieu qui l'aiment'. At any rate this blindfold romance temporarily gave Balzac one more female confidant to whom he could reveal his embarrassments and woes, lay bare his 'cœur d'enfant' whose candour and truthfulness were so ill appreciated by Ève, and show his still unsated longing for that discreet and tranquil love which, one assumes, neither Ève nor Sarah was at that moment providing. 'Pensez-vous empêcher un poète de vous rêver jeune, belle et spirituelle?' The correspondence dwindled in the summer of 1836 and ceased in the spring of 1837.

Ève, Sarah, Louise—with Henriette not entirely eliminated. If 1836 was a doleful year, it was also, from the sentimental point of view, a varied one. Another woman now appears: Mme Caroline Marbouty, a native of Limoges who had left her husband and come up to Paris, like George Sand, in the hope of making a living by her pen. In May or June she was introduced to Balzac by Jules Sandeau. He found her so companionable that when in July the Viscontis commissioned and financed him for a trip to Italy, he invited her to go with him, and she accepted with alacrity. Count Visconti's mother had just died, and someone was needed at Turin to look after his interests in the settlement of her estate. It says much for the kindness and generosity of the Viscontis that they chose Balzac for this mission. Sarah could not of course have guessed that Balzac was going to take a young woman with him, but she doubtless realized how much he needed the change of climate—his health had several times given cause for alarm—and how much his work might benefit from the experience of life in Italy.

Balzac and Caroline set out in a post-chaise at the end of July, and whether through romantic exuberance or because they naïvely thought to avoid scandal in this way, she donned male attire provided by Buisson and posed as his secretary 'Marcel'. They arrived at Turin on July 31st. We cannot doubt that Balzac enjoyed having a pretty woman with him, although from Caroline's own account of the escapade it is clear that he was in no mood for a *grande passion*. Possibly she was disappointed at this, but as his 'secretary', she had the pleasure of mixing with the exalted people to whose circles Balzac had made sure of being admitted by providing himself with introductions from Paris. The masquerade was transparent; the explanation Balzac gave to a friendly nobleman of Turin was that Marcel's virtue was safe since he himself was deeply in love with another woman. Such a guarantee, coming from Balzac, had dubious value.

Legal delays prevented him from settling the Visconti affair, but his stay in Italy was pleasant and refreshing. His reputation as a writer was already established in Piedmont, and the three weeks he spent there were filled with agreeable and flattering relationships. He had already known in Paris some distinguished Italians, such as Princess Belgiojoso and Count and Countess Sanseverino. Among celebrities he now met may be mentioned the writer Silvio Pellico. The two travellers returned to France via the Simplon and Geneva, and one of Balzac's earliest tasks on his return to Chaillot was, while reviving sweet memories of his sojourn with Ève at Geneva, to give her as disarming an account as possible of the way he had spent the last five weeks.

But he also had to tell her news which caused him great grief—the death of Mme de Berny during his absence. His underlying loyalty to her, a spiritual loyalty, had never faltered even when he neglected her, and the despondency caused by this loss was increased by a host of troubles which for a time he had been able to leave behind him. One of them was a new outbreak of jealousy in September on Ève's part: she had at last got wind of Sarah. Another was the distress in which his mother found herself, chiefly through the help she had given to her favourite son Henri, the ne'er-do-well, who, after three years in Mauritius, had returned to France in 1834 with a wife. They were both penniless, and, with the child born to them in 1835, remained on the hands of the Balzac family until and after they were shipped back to the Indies in December 1836. Mme Balzac's special tenderness for Henri aroused some resentment in Honoré, who probably made her a model for the foolishly devoted Mme Bridau in *La Rabouilleuse:*

Vous avez donné votre cœur à un monstre en qui vous avez eu votre gloire, et vous avez méconnu celui de vos enfants en qui est votre gloire véritable!

Honoré still owed his mother money, and was finding it difficult to pay her even a meagre quarterly allowance. Laure Surville and her husband, with two daughters for whom they would eventually have to find dowries, could do little to help.

No year could pass by without some trouble with publishers. Werdet's reign was now drawing to an end. He had crippled himself in satisfying his ambition and buying out Balzac's other publishers. Now he had neither capital nor credit, and by the end of the year he was well on the way to bankruptcy. He urged Balzac to fulfil his contracts and then to settle his accounts with him; relations became acrimonious. In November Werdet consented to sell his rights in Balzac's works, and this set Balzac free to make new arrangements for delivering himself of his most urgent debts. He was lucky enough to find, through the agency of Victor Bohain, a financial syndicate with whom he made a contract which held out rosy prospects. In return for the exclusive right to publish his new work (except that already promised) and exploit his old work for fifteen years, they undertook all the expenses of publication and were to pay him one half of the net proceeds. In addition, he was to receive an initial advance of 50,000 francs and generous monthly advances provided that he furnished a stipulated number of volumes. This he was not able to do for three, let alone fifteen years, but the 50,000 francs were a windfall, and Delloye and Lecou sponsored many of his publications until 1838, when Souverain, Balzac's best and most congenial publisher, came forward to take their place.

This contract did not operate with sufficient rigour to suspend altogether his habit of sending certain of his stories to the newspapers before they were published in book-form, and a chance of adding to his income from this source was offered to him at the same time. The year 1836 witnessed the birth in France of the cheap press: *Le Siècle*, founded by Armand Dutacq, and *La Presse*, founded by Émile de Girardin. Their idea was to halve the usual rate of subscription by reserving considerable space for advertisements and by the publication of serial novels from the pen of popular authors, a sure means of increasing sales. Both of these journals became very useful to Balzac. He was to get on very well with Dutacq, but harmony never reigned long between Balzac and Girardin. As usual it was Delphine who tried to smooth out their disagreements. In the early months of 1836 she was busy coaxing Balzac back into her salon. In May she brought out her light fantastic novel, *La Canne de M. de Balzac*, in which, by supposing that the celebrated stick of 1834 conferred on its owner the power to make himself invisible, she paid tribute to Balzac's genius for seeing right into the hearts of men and women.

M. de Balzac, comme les princes populaires qui se déguisent pour visiter la cabane du pauvre, et les palais du riche qu'ils veulent éprouver, M. de Balzac se cache pour observer; il regarde, il regarde les gens qui se croient seuls, qui pensent comme jamais on ne les a vus penser; il observe des génies qu'il surprend au saut du lit, des sentimens en robe de chambre, des vanités en bonnet de nuit, des passions en pantoufles, des fureurs en casquettes, des désespoirs en camisoles, et puis il vous met tout cela dans un livre! . . .

He was mollified, and though he did not forbear to scold his 'écolière' for wasting her talents, he began to frequent her salon once more, and gave his mordant satire on social life in Alençon—*La Vieille Fille*—to *La Presse* in the autumn of 1836. He wrote intermittently for it until 1847, though he dealt more willingly with Girardin's editors than with the owner himself. Delphine's attachment to him remained constant. Under the name of 'Le Vicomte de Launay' she wrote the gossip column—'Le Courrier de Paris'—for her husband's newspaper, and missed no opportunity to praise and defend the great novelist.

iv. From the Rue des Batailles to Les Jardies. 1837–8

Early in 1837, Balzac made a second trip to Italy, on the same errand as before. This time the dispute between the Visconti heirs was settled by agreement. Count Guidoboni-Visconti got little enough out of it, but Balzac had looked after his interests competently; and the affair gave him another chance to elude his creditors for a space, and also to recover his health and vigour. His social successes in Milan, where he went this time, were even greater than they had been at Turin. Balzac and a purely meteorological phenomenon—the recent aurora borealis—were the talk of the town. His most frequent resort was the salon of Countess Maffei, a lady who was later to have much to do with the *Risorgimento* movement. Here he was an honoured and even a spoilt guest. In her company he visited the public monuments and art galleries, and met the sculptor Alessandro Puttinati, who did a statuette of him which, or a copy of which, very appropriately went to Sarah Visconti. Balzac was received as well by the Austrian overlords as by the aristocracy of Milan: a list of brilliant names bears witness to the conquests he made. At the Scala Theatre he was lionized. He made friends with Countess Sanseverino's brother, Prince Porcia, and the only famous person he found uncongenial was Manzoni, author of *I Promessi Sposi*, a work which he adversely criticized. In March he went on to Venice for a week. There he was less warmly received, though this did not prevent him from writing with enthusiasm about Venice, its élite and their mode of life, in *Massimila Doni*, which he began in June. His whole-hearted sympathy with the *Risorgimento*, in spite of its addiction to liberal doctrines, dates from the period of his Italian journeys. At the end of the month he began a long and devious journey home—Genoa, Florence, Milan again, Como and the Saint-Gothard.

On his return he had to resume the tiresome game of hide-and-seek with creditors. Werdet was filing his petition, and his plight affected Balzac, who had involved him in a substantial debt to Duckett. The latter, intent on recovering the uttermost farthing, had already seized Balzac's tilbury of 1831, still stored at the Rue Cassini, while its owner was away in Italy. A descent by bailiffs on the 15th February at

13 Rue des Batailles had proved abortive, thanks to Balzac's foresight in renting the place under assumed names. His official residence was, for a time, 22 Rue de Provence, where he rented a single furnished room which was not liable to distraint. He thought of taking refuge with the Carrauds, now in retirement at Frapesle, near Issoudun; but a nearer asylum came to hand—the Viscontis received him at their house in the Champs-Élysées, where he was able to give his attention to *Les Employés* and other stories.

Even here he was not safe. Duckett discovered his whereabouts and sent a bailiff disguised as a postman bringing 6,000 francs in cash to the novelist. This ruse drew Balzac from his lair and the bailiff arrested him. Happily Sarah intervened and paid off the 1,345 francs immediately required.

It was a strange situation for a prominent personality whose portrait by Louis Boulanger was even then being exhibited in the Paris Salon; who, in May, in resplendent but hired garments, had attended the royal fête given at Versailles on the occasion of the Duke of Orleans' wedding; and of whom the legend ran, according to P. L. Jacob's bantering account, 'que M. de Balzac déjeune de baronnes, dîne de marquises et soupe de duchesses'.[1] A heavy bout of work at the Viscontis' house ended in another physical breakdown—inflammation of the lungs, to recover from which he spent some time at Saché in the early autumn. Since the Chaillot flat was no longer safe from persecutors, Balzac now embarked upon a new adventure—the purchase of a property between Saint-Cloud and Sèvres—the land and 'maisonnette' of Les Jardies. The railway from Paris to Versailles was being laid down, and there was to be a station at Sèvres within easy distance of the house. Balzac had to buy piece-

[1] *Le Constitutionnel*, 30 Sept. 1838.

meal the portions of land he wanted, his intention being to renovate the 'maisonnette' as a dwelling for the Viscontis, who, good souls, were providing a substantial loan towards the purchase, and to build a 'pavillon' for himself. The complete estate also contained a porter's lodge where Balzac intended to house his cook and gardener. Building operations were begun in October, and thus Balzac started to pile up fresh debts. In the meantime, although he was still in spasmodic occupation of the Chaillot flat, he took rooms elsewhere to keep the bailiffs off the scent: an apartment in Sèvres, and a room at 108 Rue de Richelieu, owned by Buisson.

In 1837 he did not publish many new novels. He was chiefly occupied in clearing off his contracts for the 'Études de Moeurs' and the 'Études Philosophiques'. But *Les deux Poètes*, in which Lucien de Rubempré makes his first appearance on Balzac's stage, and *Les Employés*, a notable attack on the French Civil Service, were no mean achievement; and he performed a remarkable feat in the late autumn. He had made a first draft of *César Birotteau* in 1834. He now re-wrote it in five days, and then corrected fifteen proofs and saw it through the press in twenty days:

—Composé en vingt jours par M. de Balzac, malgré l'imprimerie; composé en vingt jours par l'imprimerie, malgré M. de Balzac.[1]

Since the spring he had been pondering over a new way of making money. During an enforced halt at Genoa in March he had fallen in with a merchant, Giuseppe Pezzi, whose head was full of a scheme for the exploitation of the abandoned Roman silver-mines in Sardinia, the rejected dross from which was still supposed to contain a fair proportion of lead and silver ore. Balzac's imagination was fired,

[1] Lovenjoul, *H. O.*, 361: *Malheurs et aventures de César Birotteau avant sa naissance*, by Édouard Ourliac.

and in 1838 he scraped up enough money for a journey to Sardinia to look into the possibilities. He left Paris in the middle of March, took a boat from Marseilles to Ajaccio, where he had to wait a week before he could get on to a boat bound for the Sardinian port of Alghiero. Then, after further delay, he hired a horse and set out on his quest.

The picture the mind conjures up of Balzac, obese and out of condition, plodding on horseback across the rugged maquis in search of a fortune, is distressing rather than amusing. When he reached the Nurra mine in which his hope lay, he found that Pezzi had forestalled him by staking out a claim for himself: a Marseilles firm was already testing the ore. There were other mines on the island, and the prospects for exploitation were far from nugatory. In fact mining for lead and silver in Sardinia became a prosperous concern in the second half of the century, under the aegis of the newly-unified government of Italy. Balzac's misfortune was that he was incompetent in such matters. He had borrowed another person's idea, taken no steps to discover what the real situation was, and had no mining engineer or analyst with him to give an expert opinion. The result was another sharp disappointment, which he solaced by a new visit to Milan, where he stayed for over a month with Prince Porcia on a sight-seeing holiday. He returned to Paris in June. He was soon to be absorbed in preparations for occupying Les Jardies; but he was also beginning another love-affair.

He was still corresponding with Ève, though relations with her were uneasy. His letters in 1837 suggest discouragement, but he still deems it worth while to allay her suspicions about other women, or even to forestall them. In March 1838, after spending a few days at Nohant with George Sand, he is at pains to convince her that George is too mannish to inspire love. His letters are full of complaints about his unhappy situation and information about his writings; but in the main they describe his experiences, comment upon literary and artistic events and give his opinions on other writers. Such was the state of things when, in 1838, he turned his attention to Mme Hélène de Valette. This attachment began in the usual way—by an exchange of letters—probably not long after he had told Ève that

M. de Hanski est bien bon d'imaginer que les femmes s'enflamment pour les auteurs; je n'ai et n'aurai jamais rien à craindre à ce sujet.[1]

Hélène de Valette was a beautiful widow of thirty who had reverted to her maiden name. She had been brought up at Vannes in Brittany, and after her husband's death in 1828 spent a good deal of her time at Guérande, in the Loire-Inférieure. It seems that Balzac joined her there in June or July 1838, and that subsequently, for a year or two, they used to take one or two weeks' summer holiday there together. Also, during her frequent sojourns in Paris, she used to ride out to Les Jardies on horseback, attired in Breton costume. In accordance with his curious habit, Balzac knew her as 'Marie', and they exchanged a tender correspondence, little of which is at present accessible. The visits to Guérande furnished Balzac with the topographical background for *Béatrix*, which he first conceived in 1838 after his talks with George Sand had furnished him with a central theme: the liaison between the Hungarian musician Franz Liszt and the Countess d'Agoult, alias Daniel Stern. Hélène was not fanatically constant to Balzac; in 1840 he learnt from a jealous rival that she had told him fairy-stories about her status and upbringing, and their relations cooled down. But for a few years she seems to have replaced Sarah as 'la personne actuelle', to use Balzac's own term. None the less

[1] *E.*, i, 452 (20–27 Jan. 1838).

Sarah Visconti remained a very good friend, especially at moments when his need for money was urgent.

Building operations at Les Jardies were still in progress, but by July 1838 he was beginning to live there, although he still kept the rooms at Chaillot. He celebrated his move in the autumn by giving a grand dinner to his closest friends of the time: Dutacq of *Le Siècle*, Édouard Ourliac of *Le Figaro*, Gérard de Nerval, Gavarni, Léon Gozlan, Laurent-Jan and Charles Lassailly. The latter three now began to figure largely in Balzac's life. Léon Gozlan was a journalist, novelist and dramatist, of some wit and ability, but few principles. He was later to enrich our knowledge of Balzac, with embellishments, by his *Balzac en pantoufles* and his *Balzac chez lui*. Laurent-Jan was a desultory journalist with a sardonic turn of wit: Ève in 1850 was to find him 'insupportable, emporté, capricieux et du plus mauvais ton'. Balzac probably took to him because of the contrast between his industrious self and this unconventional, café-haunting idler and tattler: but they were both interested in drama. Charles Lassailly, whom in 1839 Balzac installed for a time at Les Jardies, was an unbalanced young Bohemian who had made some sporadic efforts at writing, and whom Balzac selected as a likely aid for his theatre projects. In return for food and lodging, he was to hold himself at the great man's disposition for the provision of ideas for plays and the composition of the dialogue. According to Gozlan, Balzac used to pounce on him at all hours of the night, demanding material or inspiration. He did not for long resist the wear-and-tear of this one-sided collaboration with genius, decamped from Les Jardies, and eventually died mad.

When Balzac moved to Les Jardies, it was a very uncomfortable house. In order to have good large rooms in his 'pavillon', he had been driven to the fantastic device of building an outside staircase. When he brought his furniture from Chaillot he had it stored in the 'maisonnette', where the Viscontis came to live at intervals in 1839 and 1840. There it was relatively safe from distraint. In the meantime his imagination supplied any deficiency in decoration and furnishings, and Gozlan records that he scrawled up on the walls, in charcoal, the indications of what he would have liked to have:

Ici un revêtement en marbre de Paros . . . Ici un stylobate en bois de cèdre. . . . Ici un plafond peint par Eugène Delacroix. . . . Ici une tapisserie d'Aubusson, etc.

This was the first house he had ever owned, though his tenure was very precarious, for the expenses he incurred in building and maintaining it were far beyond his capacity to pay.

The eccentricity of his arrangements has supplied much humorous material for biographers. So have his eccentricities of conduct during the two years of his stay at Les Jardies: the feasts he gave, the pranks with cronies, his nocturnal perambulations, the feuds with neighbours, the trouble he had over the maintenance of his boundary-walls which, thanks to the shifting soil, were perpetually falling down; also the crazy schemes for enrichment which took shape in his head when he gazed at the land surrounding the house. Cognate with such extravagances is the foundation of the 'Société du Cheval Rouge' which may plausibly be assigned to the year 1838. This was partly a dining-club which took its name from the modest Paris inn where the first meetings were held, and partly a mutual aid society. The members had to be journalists on the staffs of leading newspapers, and each of them swore to sing the praises and further the careers of his fellow-members. The associates whom Balzac chose were Gozlan, Gautier, Nerval, Merle, editor of *La*

Quotidienne, Alphonse Karr, Louis Desnoyers and others of the profession. Secret societies appealed greatly to the unsuppressed boy in Balzac. Gangsterism at different social levels is given an important place in such novels as *L'Histoire des Treize*, *La Rabouilleuse*, and *Splendeurs et misères des courtisanes*. He drew great satisfaction from arranging the meetings of the 'Chevaux Rouges', moving them from one 'stable' (i.e. restaurant) to another, and laying down absurd rules for the preservation of secrecy. After a few sessions, so Gautier affirms, the Society perished because its members could not afford the dinners. Alphonse Karr gives it a few months of life, Gozlan several years.

Balzac was not completely established at Les Jardies until July 1839, and he only remained there until December 1840. It was inconvenient to be living so far away from publishers and printers. On the other hand, in spite of relaxations such as those mentioned above, occasional onsets of fatigue, and mishaps like the sprain which (so he told Ève) kept him in bed for forty days in the summer of 1839, life at Les Jardies gave him good opportunity for prolonged work. 1838 had witnessed the appearance of his second study of social rivalries in Alençon—*Le Cabinet des antiques*, his lively exposure of financial roguery in *La Maison Nucingen*, and his first full-length portrait of the Bohemian type of journalist in *Une Fille d'Ève*[1]. 1839 was a remarkably productive year. The first two parts of *Béatrix* added Camille Maupin, the authoress modelled on George Sand, to the list of outstanding Balzacian characters. The second part of *Illusions perdues*[2] brought the ambitious poetaster Lucien de Rubempré to Paris, and gave his creator ample scope for deriding and castigating the whole confraternity

---

[1] *Le Siècle*, 31 Dec., continued until 14 Jan. 1839.
[2] *Un grand homme de province à Paris.*

of Parisian journalists. Among other memorable writings may be cited his Italian study *Massimila Doni; Les Secrets de la Princesse de Cadignan*,[1] which develops the portrait of his second high society coquette, Diane de Maufrigneuse; and the early version of *Le Curé de village*, his second great 'Scene of Country Life'. But such a fever of effort could not remain unabated. Although there were to be no further European journeys until 1843, other distractions came to divert him from his major purpose.

v. Peytel: *Vautrin*. 1839–40

One of these distractions was the 'Peytel Affair', which has its place among the notable *causes célèbres* of the nineteenth century.

Sébastien Peytel was a notary at Belley, some fifty miles from Bourg. In 1830 he had tried his hand at journalism in Paris, and had been known to Balzac and Gavarni as a fellow contributor to *Le Voleur*. On November 1st 1838, during a nocturnal journey from Macon to Belley, he shot his wife in the carriage in which they were travelling; then he turned his attention to their man-servant Louis Rey, who had been preceding them in an open cart, and despatched him with blows from the archaeologist's hammer he was carrying with him. Such at least was the accusation brought against him at his trial at Bourg in August 1839. The question of Peytel's guilt has never been satisfactorily settled.

As a sensational event the case received much comment in the press, *more gallico*, while it was still pending. The prosecution contended that Peytel had murdered his wife for her dowry, and that he liquidated the man-servant as a witness of the crime. Peytel's defence was that Louis Rey, intent on robbery, had aimed at him and shot his wife by

[1] Then entitled *La Princesse parisienne*.

mistake; he had then done justice on Rey with his hammer. An alternative possibility, one which would have saved Peytel from the guillotine, was that Mme Peytel and Rey were lovers, and that their plans to get rid of him had miscarried. What made things easier for the prosecution was the fact that very insufficient police investigations had been made on the scene of the crime. It is unlikely that a twentieth-century jury would have condemned Peytel on the evidence, but he was found guilty and sentenced to death. He was by repute an eccentric, irascible and quarrelsome man. There were some doubts as to his integrity as a notary, and strange tales were told of his treatment of his wife during their short-lived marriage. But the several men of letters who knew him—Lamartine had attended his wedding—vigorously rejected the idea that he was a calculating murderer. Two of them, Balzac and Gavarni, took active steps as soon as the verdict was given. They obtained permission from the Ministry of the Interior to interview the condemned man at Bourg. A confidential communication he made to them convinced them both of his innocence, but Peytel forbade them to disclose it, and they had to support their appeal for revision of the case by legalistic and circumstantial arguments.

This Balzac did in his 'Lettre sur le procès de Peytel' which *Le Siècle* published on September 27th to 29th 1839. He contended that the killing could not have been premeditated, or prompted by greed: if it were so Peytel was a fool to have staged the crime when and where he did. With the ingenuity of a detective of fiction Balzac examined the scanty evidence, and argued that it pointed, not to a coldblooded assassination, but rather to 'quelque terrible drame imprévu, qui rend Peytel, non pas innocent, il avoue l'homicide de Louis Rey, mais non coupable'. In brief, Balzac was content to hint that Peytel's violence was inspired by anger at the sudden discovery of his wife's intrigue with Louis Rey. Peytel did not urge this defence, and it is clear from Balzac's allusions to the affair in his correspondence that he attributed his silence to chivalrous principles: Peytel had preferred to die rather than besmirch the honour of his wife.

Balzac's long and impassioned plea was ineffectual, and Peytel went to the guillotine. The novelist's motive in making this attempt to save the life of a former friend has of course received close scrutiny: was it self-advertisement that prompted him or a burning desire to prevent an injustice? We are entitled to judge between detractors and defenders and conclude that, although his intervention was belated and the manner of it untactful, his intentions were laudable, and that the affair does him honour. Unfortunately it robbed him of several weeks' valuable time and involved him in new expenditure. He himself asserted, with customary hyperbole, that the affair had cost him 10,000 francs in actual money, and 30,000 francs in time sacrificed. None the less, by the end of the year he had *Pierrette*, his only truly successful study of child-life, and a very poignant one, nearly ready for publication in *Le Siècle*.

Another distraction from his main work—though all critics do not regard it as such—was his now fitful, now pertinacious efforts to achieve success in the theatre. They had been temporarily abandoned in 1823, but were renewed in 1830 and after. It was in that year that he started the *Album* in which he jotted down aphorisms and ideas for plays.[1] Few of the many plays so projected were ever written. It was under the pressure of debt that his mind most readily turned to the theatre, and the idea of employing a

[1] It was published in 1910 by J. Crépet as *Pensées, sujets, fragmens* (A. Blaizot). On this subject see D. Z. Milatchitch, *Le Théâtre de H. de B.*, and *Lé Théâtre inédit de H. de B.*, Hachette, 1930.

team of collaborators, so successfully practised by such authors as Eugène Scribe, seemed to him the best means of ensuring rapid production and quick returns. In 1831 it was Victor Ratier whom he hoped to recruit; in 1834 Jules Sandeau; in 1835 his 'secretary' the Marquis de Belloy. In 1839 it was Charles Lassailly, whose credit at Les Jardies ran out after he had made an ineffectual contribution to *La première Demoiselle*. This was a play Balzac conceived in 1837, for which he wrote the scenario while at Ajaccio in March 1838, and which, by early 1839, he had strong hopes of seeing accepted for the Théâtre de la Renaissance. Under its definitive title, *L'École des ménages*, it was finished in great haste in February 1839, and had its official reading towards the end of that month. It was rejected as being too risky an undertaking for a newly-found theatre.

Having so nearly got a play on to the stage, Balzac persevered, and in the autumn of 1839 he succeeded in obtaining a contract for the production of a new one, *Vautrin*, at the Porte-Saint-Martin theatre. *Vautrin* is sheer melodrama in which the half-sinister, half-benevolent gangster imported from *Le père Goriot* shows his mettle as the resourceful protector of a fine young nobleman, deprived of his rank and heritage by a father who disowns him. This unnatural father too comes straight from a novel: *L'Enfant maudit*, though he bears a different name. The popular actor, Frédéric Lemaître, was to take the title-rôle, and the first performance was fixed for March 14th 1840.

When the time came for rehearsals, Balzac was not ready with his script. Théophile Gautier amusingly related how Balzac's first impulse was to solve the problem by collaboration. One day in late 1839 or early 1840 he received a pressing summons to attend on Balzac at his pied-à-terre in the Rue de Richelieu, and on arriving was told that he,

Ourliac, Laurent-Jan, de Belloy and Balzac himself were each to write an act by the next day. When asked to state the subject and sketch out the plan and characters, Balzac exclaimed: 'Ah! s'il faut vous conter le sujet, nous n'aurons jamais fini!' Naturally the collaborators fell down before such a task, and Balzac wrote the play with some help from Laurent-Jan. Then he found himself condemned, for a matter of two and a half months, to the strain of attending rehearsals at the Porte Saint-Martin and adapting his still incomplete drama to the exigencies of the individual actors.

In preparation for the great day Balzac himself took over the task of selling the dearer seats—boxes and stalls—to people he thought most likely to form a sympathetic audience. It was his way of avoiding the use of a professional *claque*. But he sold the tickets so long in advance that many were re-sold, and the curtain rose before an audience that was either indifferent or hostile. At the fourth act, when Lemaître, as Vautrin, appeared in the disguise of a Mexican general, and removed his hat to reveal an enormous toupée audaciously similar to the one worn by Louis-Philippe himself, there was an uproar. The heir to the throne, who was present, left the theatre to mark his disapproval of this affront to royalty. The play ended in a riot, and the next day was banned by the Ministry of the Interior.

Despite the intervention of friends, including the now influential Victor Hugo, the ban was not lifted, and Balzac had to accept as philosophically as possible what was an overwhelming defeat, made more unpalatable still by the attacks the play suffered in the newspapers—Jules Janin did not miss the opportunity to deride his old enemy. The financial consequences of that defeat were more unpleasant than the injury done to his self-esteem and reputation. He had anticipated the fruits of the hoped-for dramatic triumph.

He had raised a loan of 5,000 francs at exorbitant interest from a moneylender, Foullon, and also borrowed 10,000 francs, in all probability from Sarah Visconti, on the strength of the expected takings. A meagre compensation of 5,000 francs was offered him by the Minister of Fine Arts, but he refused it as disproportionate to the losses sustained. It says much for Balzac's invincibility of spirit that, a month or two later, he had sufficiently recovered from the cerebral neuralgia brought on by this disappointment to start negotiations for the performance of another play, *Mercadet*, at the Ambigu-Comique Theatre. He also claims to have finished *Paméla Giraud* by July 1840.

vi. *La Revue Parisienne:* Campaign for Copyright. 1840–1

The *Revue Parisienne* was Balzac's new attempt to avenge himself for the slights put upon him by certain sections of the periodical Press; also, to stand forth as a person to be reckoned with in the political world. Nor again was the idea of a quick financial return absent. In the previous year Alphonse Karr had founded his one-man satirical monthly, *Les Guêpes*, and was reaping good profits. Why should not Balzac do the same, but on a more ambitious scale, by providing in tiny format (32°) a monthly review that should vie both in quantity and quality with the existing monthlies? Dutacq, the kindly editor of *Le Siècle*, undertook to print and produce the Review. Balzac permitted himself extravagant hopes: a large circulation, and a profit of 30,000 francs a month. So *La Revue Parisienne* was launched. It was to be compact, authoritative, and cheap; one franc a number, ten francs for the yearly subscription. The Prospectus promised for each number one novel and 'literary fragments'; a letter on literature, the theatre and the arts; a topical and political commentary whose ruling principles should be concision, independence of view and fidelity to facts.

The *Revue Parisienne* ran to three numbers, published on the 25th of July, the 25th of August and the 25th of September 1840. Apart from the topical and political commentary, entitled 'Lettres Russes', deemed to be addressed to a Russian prince, and composed in collaboration with a journalist friend, Louis de Cardonne, it was indeed a one-man review. Balzac's habit was to gird up his loins a few days before the 'Review' was due to appear and give his exclusive attention to it until it had passed through the press.

These three little volumes are extremely interesting. Balzac only provided two works of fiction, one of which relates the misfortunes of a frustrated politician, the other the caprices of an aristocratic cad: Z. *Marcas* and *Les Fantaisies de Claudine*, later to be known as *Un Prince de la Bohème*; but his 'Lettres sur la littérature, le théâtre et les arts' are most valuable for a study of his literary and aesthetic ideas. They are addressed to 'la Comtesse E. . .', namely Mme Hanska, and deal with such varied authors as Latouche, Fenimore Cooper, Eugène Sue, Victor Hugo, Sainte-Beuve, Musset and Stendhal. Among Balzac's *bêtes noires*, Latouche, Sue and Louis Reybaud rank high. Sue was, in Balzac's opinion, enjoying a totally undeserved reputation and, what was more galling, making a great deal of money by it. He was soon to make even more when his *Mystères de Paris* began in *Le Constitutionnel* in 1842. Louis Reybaud, for long a contributor to the cut-throat periodical *Le Corsaire*, and now an accredited critic on the staff of the respectable daily *Le Constitutionnel*, was one of those typical journalists who exasperated Balzac, and he took the opportunity to attack him for his satirical book *Les Réformateurs modernes*, in which he had poked fun at Saint-Simon, Fourier and other socialists. So severe was Balzac to Reybaud that an unwary reader might well have ranked him with the Utopians of the age.

But Sainte-Beuve was his chief target. It was a fine chance to strike back at this declared enemy who, as recently as September 1839, had indulged in further gibes at his expense in an article entitled 'De la littérature industrielle'. Sainte-Beuve deserved some hard knocks, for he admitted himself in one of his note-books: 'Chaque critique a son gibier sur lequel il tombe et qu'il dépèce de préférence. . . . Pour moi, c'est Balzac.' The first volume of the *Histoire de Port-Royal* had just appeared, and Balzac fell on it tooth and nail. Neither the author's historical sense nor his political views were spared. The involved style and laboured metaphors which had inspired the Duchesse d'Abrantès to nickname him 'Sainte-Bévue' were mercilessly exposed, and at the same time parodied in the opening pages of *Les Fantaisies de Claudine*. Balzac was to repeat that pleasurable exercise in 1842 in *Monographie de la Presse parisienne*. On the other hand, the 'Étude sur M. Beyle', inspired by Stendhal's *Chartreuse de Parme*, ranks as the sole eulogy which that writer ever received in his life-time. Stendhal was astonished, delighted, and, on reflexion, amused by the article. The two writers were kindred spirits in spite of differences in the scope and style of their works, and Balzac was exceptional in his appreciation of Stendhal's genius.

The 'Lettres Russes' and an article of the 25th of September —'Sur les Ouvriers'—contain a vigorous and amusing exposition of Balzac's settled political views. They also launch a malicious attack upon the statesman Adolphe Thiers (and upon his mother-in-law Mme Dosne, the 'power behind the throne') for his policy with regard to the Eastern Question.

The Anglo-French misunderstanding over the destinies of Turkey and Egypt was at that time keeping Frenchmen in a fever of patriotism. Balzac (or Balzac-Cardonne) does not disguise his Anglophobia, but he shows his ability to take a calm view and to realize that Palmerston's diplomatic victory in forming the Quadruple Alliance without the participation of France was far from furnishing a *casus belli*.

All this is typical Balzac and stimulating to modern readers, but it did little to further his real interests. By the end of September eight thousand copies of the review remained unsold, and the account-books showed a deficit of 1,801 francs. Balzac again acknowledged defeat. This venture did not, thanks to Dutacq, involve him in heavy bills like the *Chronique de Paris*, but although the writing of these three numbers had been concentrated in frantic bursts of last-minute composition and correction, it must have demanded long efforts of reading and assimilation before he ever put pen to paper. The *Revue Parisienne*, like the bulk of the *Lettres à l'Étrangère*, prove that Balzac must have found time for a remarkable amount of reading in addition to his other occupations.

More pertinent to the successful prosecution of Balzac's creative work were the efforts he made between 1839 and 1841 to obtain protection for authors, and legal recognition of their rights. Since the 1789 Revolution the principle had prevailed that literary works, once published, became public property. This put authors at a great disadvantage for the exploitation of their works, and although they could protect themselves to some extent by carefully conceived contracts —Balzac was a recognized adept at this—at death they could only pass on their rights to their heirs for a variable but limited period. Nor was there any international convention about copyright. Balzac himself suffered greatly from the piracy of foreign, mostly Belgian publishers, who reprinted his novels, without paying him a penny, as soon as they came out, and sometimes even before they had appeared in book form. A similar piracy was practised in the French provinces, where local newspapers reproduced works appearing in the Parisian press, without seeking authorization and without incurring any expense. A like brigandage could be carried on within the country by theatre-directors and literary parasites, for if a novel was adapted as a play, or vice versa, the original author could claim no share in the proceeds. Added to this was another grievance against which Balzac had been protesting since 1830: the slipperiness of less reputable publishers in their financial dealings with authors. This was made possible by the established system of credit: a publisher paid his author, his printer and his paper-manufacturer in bills of exchange to fall due at some future date. His payees, if they wished to realize their assets immediately, had to negotiate these bills at a discount. Now between the date of issue and the date when they fell due, all sorts of vicissitudes might occur. The publisher's business might for instance perceptibly droop or he might even become insolvent, and the commission levied by the discounters would vary according to their assessment of the drawer's solvency. It follows that the value of the 'effet à échéance' might dwindle considerably in the course of its negotiation. Balzac had already aired this grievance in an article of March 1830.[1] He returned to the attack in *Un grand homme de province à Paris*, published in June 1839.

The whole situation was unsatisfactory, and Balzac had frequently claimed that the rights of an author in his works should be acknowledged as genuine and transmissible

---

[1] 'De l'état actuel de la Librairie', in *Feuilleton des Journaux politiques*.

property. In a 'Lettre adressée aux écrivains français du XIXe siècle',[1] and an article 'Sur les questions de la propriété littéraire et de la contrefaçon',[2] he had proposed the foundation of an association of authors to protect their mutual interests, and the establishment of an international agreement regarding copyright. Such an association was evidently needed; but ironically enough, Balzac himself was not consulted when, in April 1838, a group of prominent writers founded the 'Société des Gens de Lettres' in response to that need. He was not even invited to join. The prime mover was Louis Desnoyers, and the original membership included such men as Victor Hugo, Dumas, Lamennais, Gozlan, etc. At the end of the year, when faced with a particularly outrageous example of Belgian piracy (twenty pirated editions of *César Birotteau*), Balzac applied to the Société for admission. He was elected through the influence of Gozlan, and his impetuous activity soon made itself felt in committee work. In August 1839 he succeeded Villemain as President. In October of that year he made a telling speech before the Rouen tribunal when the Société sued the *Mémorial de Rouen* for lifting articles. After the expiration in January 1840 of his term as President (he was succeeded by Victor Hugo, and by normal procedure became Vice-President) he was still fertile in projects. In May 1840 he submitted to the Société a *Code Littéraire* which was not adopted and had to wait until 1862 to be published.[3]

A year later, when a commission of the Chambre des Députés was appointed to investigate the question, and when the Société was preparing a memorandum to set before the Chamber, Balzac drew up his own proposals in a brochure entitled *Notes remises à MM les Députés formant*

---

[1] *Revue de Paris*, Nov. 1834.
[2] *Chronique de Paris*, 30 Oct. 1836.   [3] By Gozlan, in *Balzac chez lui*.

la commission de la loi sur la propriété littéraire. Unfortunately the proposal for a bill was dropped, and it fell to
Napoleon III to promulgate a new law of copyright in 1854.
Balzac's remedies for the prevalent evil varied a little from
one moment to another. In a letter to *La Presse* of August
1839 he proposed the establishment of a State fund to buy
out author's rights at so much a volume. In *Notes remises* . . .
he marshalled cogent arguments to prove that literary property should be enjoyed in perpetuity. In his *Code Littéraire* he
gave the greater part of his attention to the matter of contracts with publishers, and proposed that they should be
made under the surveillance of the Société. He also stipulated for an equitable apportionment of rights in the case of
works written in collaboration, offered a statement of principles regarding the thorny questions of plagiarism and
translation, and even made proposals for the protection of
authors against unscrupulous criticism.

There was scarcely a clause in this *Code Littéraire* which
was not prompted by some actual experience he had had in
his dealings with publishers, editors and printers. Yet his
proposals met with little response, and before long he grew
impatient with the Société for its sluggishness and inaction.
He resigned his membership in the autumn of 1841, and
though this was not accepted he ceased to take any further
interest in its sessions until 1848. His fellow-members probably felt it hard to adjust themselves to his domineering
personality, but no-one was more *au fait* with the subject
than he, and the 'Société des Gens de Lettres' owes its
existence in great measure to him.

vii. From Les Jardies to the Rue Basse. 1840–1

Since Balzac had so many irons in the fire, it is no wonder
that in August 1840 we find Souverain, now his main pub-

lisher, threatening him with legal proceedings for failure to keep contract; that in the same month Dujarier, director of *La Presse* and a good friend of Balzac, is complaining of not having received any copy from him for a year; that in October one of Souverain's printers exclaims: 'M. de Balzac est un auteur à ne jamais imprimer.' But pressure from publishers and editors was less embarrassing than the persecutions of creditors.

Not that all of these caused Balzac anxiety. Some of his debts he classified as 'tranquilles', since they were owed to well-wishers who were not in a hurry for their money: for instance, his old friends Dablin, Mme Delannoy and the tailor Buisson. To the latter, by 1840, he owed 12,000 francs for clothes alone, and was shielded by him from rival creditors with that interested solicitude which, as Panurge maintains in argument with Pantagruel, a lender always feels for a borrower. Repayments to the Viscontis were never urgently reclaimed, but the debt to his mother, dating back to 1828, although it seems to have been reduced by now, was by no means a 'tranquil' one, for he was supposed to make her an allowance by way of interest.

The more urgent debts were those he had more recently contracted. After 1838 the formidable expenses for Les Jardies came to swell his liabilities: repeated purchases of land and accounts sent in by contractors and tradesmen. Even towards the close of 1839 there were two attempts at distraint at Les Jardies, and he described himself to Ève as being 'traqué comme un lièvre'. In the winter of 1839–40 came the new debts contracted on account of *Vautrin*, particularly the loan obtained from the rapacious Foullon. By 1840 his *Chronique de Paris* liabilities still amounted to 10,000 francs, and by the end of that year his total indebtedness, which in 1831 had been about 50,000 francs, and which had increased steadily year by year, was well over the quarter-million mark.

In June 1840, Ruffin, who had sold him some land and the porter's lodge at Les Jardies, sent in the bailiffs for non-payment of the purchase price. From August to September other distraints were made on Foullon's initiative. Balzac could still save his furniture by pretending that it belonged to the accommodating Viscontis. But it was becoming clear that Les Jardies had to be sold, and late in 1840 a friendly lawyer, Gavault, undertook the difficult task of putting Balzac's finances in order. Foullon pressed for the enforced sale of Les Jardies, and in July 1841 it was put up to auction and sold. But the buyer was an architect named Claret, a 'man of straw' who undertook to hold it in reserve for Balzac himself. For the latter was by no means resigned to the surrender of a property which, he averred, had cost him 100,000 francs, and for which the official selling-price was 17,500 francs. Thanks to this operation, he found himself for several years in the unenviable position of still owing sums for the original purchase and structural operations, and also of having to find the money to pay Claret. At all events Les Jardies was out of the question as a domicile. By the end of November 1840 he had left it to take up residence at Passy, at 19 Rue Basse. His 'pied à terre' in the Rue Richelieu was no longer available, for the premises had changed hands, and the new owner distrained on his furniture to pay for the rent.

The house at Passy, which is now set apart as the Balzac museum, was his last residence but one in or near Paris. Although it was too far from the centre to be really convenient, it offered a useful means for evading creditors, for it had two entrances, the one in the Rue Basse (now Rue Raynouard) and the other, at a lower level, in the Rue du

Roc (now Rue Berton). While the front entrance was being watched he could descend to the lower floor and slip out by the Rue du Roc exit. As formerly at Chaillot, a password was necessary for his friends to gain admission. And again the house was not leased in his own name, but in that of a Mlle Louise Breugniot, who lived with Balzac for many years to come under the name of Mme de Brugnol—as his house-keeper, and probably too as his mistress. The first of these employments was more than a domestic one, for this former mistress of Latouche was an educated woman, had literary friends (Frédéric Soulié, for instance, and the poetess Mme Desbordes-Valmore) and much business acumen. She was of great service to Balzac, not only in circumventing creditors, but also as a go-between with printers and publishers. If, as is usually supposed, Balzac's new 'gouvernante' also supplied his more intimate wants, she was the last known rival of Ève. It was to be expected that her eventual eclipse in favour of the Polish countess would cause some trouble and anxiety.

At this time, however, Balzac's relations with Ève were weakening still more perceptibly than they had done in 1837. During 1838 and 1839 his correspondence with Zulma Carraud was also drooping: he had paid his last visit to Frapesle in February 1838. But the topics he discussed in the few letters he did write to Zulma throw some light on his thoughts about Ève. He had never entirely ruled out the possibility of finding a wife in France: now the idea came quite frequently to his mind.

Une femme de trente ans qui aurait trois ou quatre cent mille francs et qui voudrait de moi, pourvu qu'elle fût douce et bien faite [admirable summary of *desiderata*!] me trouverait prêt à l'épouser; elle payerait mes dettes, et mon travail en cinq ans l'aurait remboursée.

So he wrote in September 1838.[1] The next month a letter to

[1] *Z. C.*, 252.

his sister reveals, in less concrete terms, the same preoccupation. In November 1839 he was urging Zulma to
arrange an advantageous marriage for him, though this
time he demanded a younger partner—of twenty-two.
Zulma reacted sadly to this exhibition of cupidity; but it
seems excusable if one turns to the Hanska correspondence of
the same period.

Early in 1839 he was writing sad and bitter letters to Ève,
and wondering again whether she was not minded to end
their correspondence. On June 2nd he exclaimed: 'Je vous
ai haïe pendant deux jours.' From August to December he
wrote only one letter—in instalments as was his custom.
On January 20th 1840, he complained of not having heard
from her for three months. 'Ah! je vous trouve excessive-
ment petite', he wrote in February on learning that her
silence was due to the infrequency of his own letters.

> Eh bien, elles étaient rares parce que je n'ai pas toujours eu l'argent
> pour les affranchir, et que je ne voulais pas vous le dire. Oui, ma détresse
> a été jusque-là, et au delà. . . . Oui, j'ai eu des jours où j'ai fièrement
> mangé un petit pain sur les boulevards.[1]

It is gratifying to see that at this stage he had sufficient
spirit to write well of Sarah Visconti, to admit that he had
dedicated *Béatrix* to her, and to commend her in warm
tones. Had he maintained such a tone of loyalty to his best
friends we should owe greater respect to him.

But, however strongly he might react to Ève's reproaches,
he still held on to the increasingly tenuous line of hope, and
on May 15th he began to run Sarah down, in company with
all Englishmen and Englishwomen. The year of *Vautrin* is
the year when, in moments of sickness and despair, he conceived the absurd idea of emigrating and seeking his fortune in Brazil. The threat of this actually did evoke some

[1] *E.*, i, 527.

response from Ève when, in July, he wrote of the project as being almost settled: in October he promised not to take any 'extreme resolution' without having seen her again. Indeed his best resource would have been to go out to Wierzchownia to regain his ascendancy over her. But how much better it would have been for him if he had found that 'femme de trente ans' who would have taken charge of him—such women have existed of all time—put up with his faults and whims, and given him at any rate the five years' tranquillity he needed! The drawback to this would have been that by that time he would have run through all her money.

He wrote only six letters to Ève in 1840, and in 1841 only five. 'Je travaille immensément et j'ai à peine le temps de vous écrire.'[1] Indeed, 1841 is the year of three full novels and one shorter story,[2] and of three others either completed, continued or begun.[3] Compared with the one novel, *Pierrette*, the three *nouvelles* published in 1840,[4] this is a noteworthy accomplishment. But hard-pressed as he was, with greater encouragement he would certainly have found time to pour out his soul to the 'chère comtesse'. Yet there are signs of a revival of hope in this latter year. He still thought it worth while to defend himself against calumnies, those for instance which were being circulated by Ève's own brother, Adam Rzewuski. And since reason was of little avail, he took consolation from superstition. He had dreamt of her, he wrote, on the 31st May. In July he consulted a fortune-teller, the 'sorcier' Balthazar, and the cards promised that in six weeks he would receive a letter which would change the course of his life. It is not

[1] *E.*, i, 551, March 1841.
[2] *Une ténébreuse Affaire, Ursule Mirouet, Mémoires de deux jeunes mariées, La fausse Maîtresse.*
[3] *Le Curé de village*; *Les Lecamus*, later to form Part I of *Sur Catherine de Médicis*; *Les deux Frères*, the first part of *La Rabouilleuse*.
[4] *Pierre Grassou, Z. Marcas, Un Prince de la Bohème.*

merely by coincidence that, in the summer months of this
year, he was reaffirming his belief in the occult by preparing *Ursule Mirouet* for the press. In September he complained of having had no letter for ten months, and she
informed him, in what was evidently an affectionately reproachful reply, that she had indeed written letters, but
that they had been returned undelivered. Thanks perhaps
to the fortune-teller, his mood became more sanguine.

J'ai *foi* dans l'année prochaine, et crois fermement que Dieu récom-
pensera tant de travaux, tant de constance et tant d'ennuis supportés.[1]

No doubt also he felt some jubilation over the fact that, in
October 1841, the final contract had been signed for the
publication of the 'Comédie Humaine' in sixteen volumes.

He had at last some cause for satisfaction on several scores.
True, he had also cause for self-reproach. Many times, in
distress, his mother had called to him for succour, and being
unable to help her in any other way, he lodged her for some
time in early 1841 at his new apartments in the Rue Basse
—not for long, because he found it impossible to endure her
changeable moods. His growing neglect, through the years,
of Zulma Carraud had culminated in his inability to find
time to see her even when, in March 1840, she was at Versailles putting her son Yorick to school. On the other hand,
his friendship with Sarah Visconti, Delphine de Girardin
and George Sand remained undisturbed. He had an occasionally useful friend in Victor Hugo, who had stood by him
over *Vautrin*, who in June 1841 provided him with tickets
of admission for his reception into the French Academy, and
unsuccessfully appealed to him to dissuade *Le Charivari*
from publishing a hostile article on that occasion. Above all,
he could feel that, in spite of the follies of the past, his
affairs were moving on to a firmer foundation, thanks to the

[1] *E.*, i, 570.

devotion of Gavault. Although he stood on the verge of bankruptcy, he announced his intention to persevere 'dans cette grande et noble tâche: payer ses dettes'.

His prospects were in fact looking better, if only for the moment. Perhaps it was because Ève felt herself to be on the threshold of release from marriage to Hanski that her letter of September 1841 had been marked by 'assurances of long-standing affection'. Her husband died two months later. Balzac learnt this on the fifth of January 1842. The letter he wrote to her on this occasion was couched in appropriately delicate terms, but it did not hide the fact that he now expected her to seal the bargain they had made seven years before at Neuchâtel. He sat back for a time in happy expectation:

Voici vingt jours que je dors tous les jours quatorze heures et que ma tête se refuse à tout travail d'esprit. Mon intelligence sommeille, tandis que mon cœur existe par tous ses fibres, et que je vis de la vie que j'aurai dans un an, par avance. Une puissance mystérieuse me jette malgré moi dans le bonheur.[1]

Thus he wrote on January 20th 1842.

[1] *E.*, ii, 6.

IV

THE FINAL STRUGGLE, 1842–50

*Ce cher M. de Balzac prétend qu'un homme
n'est complet, véritablement complet qu'avec
sept femmes, dont voici l'énumération: 1° la
femme du foyer; 2° la femme du cœur; 3° la
femme de l'esprit; 4° la femme du ménage
(qui marque le linge, a soin de la maison, etc.);
5° la femme des caprices et des folies; 6° la
femme qu'on déteste; et 7°, enfin, la femme
que l'on guette, après laquelle on court toujours
et qu'on n'a jamais, jamais.*

'Correspondance de Liszt et de la Comtesse
d'Agoult 1833–1840', published by Daniel
Ollivier, 1933, p. 97.

i. The racing quill

THE DESIRE to urge the meritoriousness of so long an
attachment was not lacking among the motives that
prompted him to begin work in April on *Albert Savarus*,
which idealizes the story of his early relations with Ève.
Was it also the presentiment of further tribulations that
inspired him to carry the novel through to a lamentable
conclusion? At any rate it soon became abundantly clear
that the felicity he longed for depended on the continuance
and even the augmentation of his creative effort. He was
still hoping to achieve great things in the realm of the
theatre. He himself had no doubts about his talent as a
dramatist. He tried again, in March 1842, to make the
theatre-going public share his conviction: with *Les Res-
sources de Quinola* at the Odéon. To win laughter and admiration of his wit he created a new Figaro, the Quinola of

the title. To provoke thought he pretended that steam-propulsion had been applied by a sixteenth-century Spaniard and that the event was more important than either Renaissance or Reformation. To provoke tears he imagined his hero, the inventor of the steamship, harried and swindled by persecutors and rivals, and robbed of his beloved by a courtesan. An anachronistic extravaganza to which, on the first night, the customarily rowdy audience of the Odéon gave no quarter. Yet it ran for nineteen performances.

To this unhappy experiment posterity owes some sprightly, perhaps spurious, anecdotes related by Gozlan. What he says about the trial reading before the theatre-committee bears out what Gautier wrote of a private reading of *Mercadet* at Les Jardies a year or so before: Balzac had enviable powers of mimicry and declamation.

Il lisait surtout avec une grande conviction; il s'abandonnait, il faisait pleurer, il faisait rire, pleurant et riant lui-même. . . . Dans le rire particulièrement il saisissait, il entraînait; il vous attelait, pour ainsi dire, à sa grosse gaîté, à quatre roues, et quoi qu'on en eût, il fallait le suivre, sauf ensuite à distraire de la part qu'on avait un peu trop largement faite à l'ouvrage, la part à laquelle avait droit le lecteur.[1]

Unfortunately his verve deserted him when he came to the fifth act, as yet unwritten, which he had to improvise. After the reading, in order to avoid divulging the secret of his address, he proposed to the theatre-director the adoption of a strange method for giving him notice of rehearsals. A messenger, armed with a missive,

se rendra chaque matin aux Champs-Élysées. . . . Quand il sera au rond-point de la fontaine . . . il se dirigera vers l'arc de l'Étoile; et, au vingtième arbre à gauche, il verra un homme qui fera semblant de chercher un merle dans les branches. . . . Votre garçon de théâtre s'approchera de cet homme et lui dira: *Je l'ai!* Cet homme lui répondra: *Puisque vous l'avez, qu'attendez-vous?* Sur cette réponse, votre garçon

---

[1] *Balzac en pantoufles*, p. 205 (modern composite edition, Delmas).

lui donnera le bulletin de répétition et s'en ira sans regarder derrière lui. . . .[1]

As with *Vautrin* in 1840, Balzac tried to secure a distinguished and well-disposed audience for the first night by taking over the sale of tickets. He overreached himself as before, and at the eleventh hour a professional *claque* had to be hired. Gozlan also finds amusement in the fact that, long after the first performance was over, Balzac was discovered fast asleep in one of the boxes. But there is pathos too in this: exhaustion from the effort he had made was stronger than the disappointment that faced him. The press reviews were mostly hostile, and he persuaded himself that even loyal supporters like Delphine de Girardin and Victor Hugo were secretly intriguing for the failure of the play.

Eighteen months later, in September 1843, another play by Balzac came before the public, this time at the Gaieté Theatre: *Paméla Giraud*. It was pruned and shortened by two practised dramatists, Bayard and Jaime, and Gavault, the manager of Balzac's finances, must have made the arrangements, for the author was then in Russia with Mme Hanska. Such a play should have pleased the socialists at any rate, for it extols the virtues of a working-class girl by contrast with the hard selfishness of the well-to-do. It ran to twenty-one performances. Reviewing it in *Le Journal des Débats*, Jules Janin, who as a rule gave no quarter either to Balzac the novelist or Balzac the playwright, damned the latter in favour of the former. 'Fines comédies, esquisses délicates, ingénieux scalpels, narration attachante, beaux petits sentiers découverts dans les ténèbres du cœur humain. Pourquoi donc, après tant d'éclat, cette misère? Pourquoi ce suicide?'[2] It is not difficult to agree with Janin in view of the

---

[1] *Ibid.*, p. 212–13.
[2] *J. des Débats*, 2 Oct., 1843. Quoted by Milatchitch, p. 166.

fact that, by 1843, the historical novel, *Sur Catherine de Médicis*, and *La Rabouilleuse*, the starkest of Balzac's provincial studies, were complete, that *Honorine, la Muse du Département* and the third part of *Illusions perdues* were in print, and, above all, that some half-dozen volumes of the 'Comédie Humaine' were out.

Indeed the contract for the publication of the 'Comédie Humaine', the issue of the Prospectus in April 1842, and the publication in July of Balzac's remarkable manifesto, the *Avant-Propos*, mark a climax in his career as a writer.

Quatre hommes (he was to write in 1844) auront eu une vie immense: Napoléon, Cuvier, O'Connell, et je veux être le quatrième. Le premier a vécu de la vie de l'Empire; il s'est inoculé des armées! Le second a épousé le globe! Le troisième s'est incarné un peuple! Moi, j'aurai porté une société toute entière dans ma tête![1]

As the revelation of a long-cherished ambition, now sponsored as much by the social scientist in Balzac (nay even the social *zoologist*)[2] as by the social historian and philosopher of 1834, the announcement of the 'Comédie Humaine' was a memorable gesture. As an event in his personal life, it was almost as much a business affair as the attempt to launch plays. Besides bringing him in an immediate 15,000 francs for the reduction of his debts—he had arranged with Gavault that proceeds from publishers, as opposed to income from periodicals, were to be devoted to this purpose—it added a great deal to the magnitude of his labours. The sixteen volumes announced consisted of 500 folio sheets of close print. Using the original editions as a manuscript, he read and corrected these sheets as well as two more proofs, and he calculated in December 1842 that he would have to

[1] *E.*, ii, 301.
[2] 'La société ne fait-elle pas de l'homme, suivant les milieux où son action se déploie, autant d'hommes différents qu'il y a de variétés en zoologie?'—*Avant-Propos*, Conard I, xxvi.

devote 200 hours a month to this special task. This calculation, however, was made at a time when he hoped to get the whole edition out in two years. Many circumstances intervened to prevent him from revising so swiftly while writing fresh novels, and it took five years, i.e. until 1846, to bring out the sixteen volumes. In May 1843 Balzac told Mme Hanska that the sales were going well: 1800 copies up to date. But clearly this was not kept up in the following years, and Balzac attributed this to inadequate advertisement. When publication was nearing completion (a seventeenth volume was to be added in 1848), the original editors, Hetzel and Furne, sold out to a new one, Houssiaux; a large number of copies remained in stock, and a deficit of 6,793 francs was disclosed. So that Balzac drew no more than the original 15,000 francs from the enterprise. He none the less, in 1845, planned a new and enlarged edition in twenty-six volumes (itself a reduction of his 1843 estimate of thirty-two volumes) and drew up a Catalogue of the works it was to contain.

At the end of 1841, by a rough-and-ready computation, Balzac had already written two-thirds of his major novels, as well as the great majority of his shorter stories. But he still had many important ones to write, most of which were to find their way into volumes of the 'Comédie Humaine' after he had, as usual, taken the gloss off them and made some living expenses out of them by selling them first of all to such periodicals as *La Presse, Le Siècle, Le Messager, Le Musée des Familles, Le Journal des Débats* and *Le Constitutionnel*. As often as not they were also published separately in book-form, Balzac's aim being now a three-fold exploitation of each of his new productions. The relatively poor sales of the 'Comédie Humaine' itself may be partly due to this fact.

He continued to arrange his undertakings in such a way as to find himself pulled in different directions at one and the same time by his various publishers and editors. Until 1845 Hetzel was his point of contact with the group of publishers concerned with the 'Comédie Humaine', and Hetzel, with whom he had very friendly relations for several years, drew him aside a little from his main endeavour by inducing him to make contributions to miscellaneous volumes: *Scènes de la vie privée et publique des animaux* (1841–2), *Le Livre des petits enfants* (1843), and *Le Diable à Paris* (1844–5). Another publisher, Maresq, elicited from Balzac, in 1843, his mock-treatise of 'social natural history', entitled *Monographie de la Presse Parisienne*, which satirically describes the genera and sub-genera of the 'ordre gendelettre' and deals some telling blows at his enemies Sainte-Beuve and Jules Janin. Souverain continued to be an important publisher for Balzac, but the relations between the two were worsening. Souverain had for long been firm and tactful with Balzac, though he had the usual difficulties: Balzac's delays in producing copy, his substitution of one work for another, his habit of abandoning an unfinished novel in order to embark on a new one. Balzac's counter-charge was that Souverain held back proofs and delayed publication of certain works. 'Vous vous souciez d'un livre comme un épicier de ses pruneaux', he had already written to him in 1839. Bickerings went on intermittently, with occasional threats of legal proceedings on both sides. Balzac's impatience grew, and by 1844 he had practically shaken free of him. As Balzac's publisher Souverain had lasted longer than any others. He came back into view in 1848 as a patient and benevolent friend always ready to do Balzac a service.

In November 1842 Balzac became involved with a supposed publisher named Locquin, a banker from the small town of Lagny, some eight miles east of Paris. The contract with Locquin, who was really acting for Dumont, was for three works which were to bring Balzac 10,000 francs, and the printing was to be done at Lagny, at a press which was driven by water-power and therefore was slow and in-efficient. Hence Balzac's frequent references to the 'miller of Lagny'. He got behind with this contract as usual and at length had practically to live at the Lagny press, working day and night, in June and July 1843, in order to complete the third part of *Illusions Perdues* and the first part of *Splendeurs et misères des courtisanes*. This was such a strain that it is generally supposed to have been a decisive factor in the break-down of his health. Then, when this slavery was all over, Locquin, stung by the size of Balzac's proof-bills, refused to pay him his due until these had been settled. The rhyme 'Loquin-coquin' became too tempting to resist. There ensued a succession of wrangles, in which Souverain also was involved, until the autumn of 1844, when yet another publisher, De Potter, was called in to take matters out of the hands of Locquin, Dumont and Souverain. In the meantime, 1843 saw Balzac in negotiation with an even less satisfactory publisher than Locquin, an adventurous Polish count, Chlen-dowski, with no capital behind him. In spite of warnings from Mme Hanska, who had heard bad things of Chlen-dowski, Balzac made contracts with him for *Modeste Mignon* and other books, found him evasive and tricky, cried out against him, swore he would have no more to do with him, but continued relations with him until 1848. For a long time the Chlendowskis were on calling terms with Mme de Brugnol.

Nor is there much change in the pattern of his dealings with newspaper-editors. He was always slow in providing copy for such periodicals as *Le Siècle*, which in 1841 had come under less genial management than that of Dutacq, now a ruined man. With *La Presse* he had many sharp exchanges, although from 1840 until his death in a duel (1845), the director Dujarier was patient with Balzac. Behind Dujarier loomed at intervals the uncongenial figure of Émile de Girardin, whom Balzac continued to hate despite the attentions and hospitality with which Delphine de Girardin continued to soothe him.

For many years his failure to produce *Les Paysans*, promised and in part paid for in 1840, kept Girardin's temper simmering, so much the more because other novels promised and actually delivered to *La Presse*[1] were almost always late. *Les Paysans* hung fire, but at last Balzac managed to send in the first part of it, under the title *Qui a terre, a guerre*, in December 1844. The text was unpolished and badly printed, and it did not please the subscribers to that newspaper. Whether because of this, or in order to do Alexandre Dumas a favour, Girardin announced the postponement of the rest of *Les Paysans* and put *La Reine Margot* in its place. Balzac leapt under the insult, and in 1845 Girardin worried him in vain for the second part of *Les Paysans*. All he could extract by the end of the year was some fragments of *Petites Misères de la vie conjugale*. The conflict, which was rendered more acrimonious by Balzac's demand for, and Girardin's refusal of higher pay, went on intermittently until July 1847. Then an insulting letter from Girardin decided Balzac to break finally with *La Presse* and pay back the advances he had received for *Les Paysans*. But this restitution was not completed until 1848.

ii. The beginnings of decline

Balzac's inability to discharge such contracts, and to make progress with other works like *Le Député d'Arcis* and *Les*

---

[1] The two parts of *La Rabouilleuse*, *Mémoires de deux jeunes mariées*, *Honorine*, *Gaudissart II*, etc.

petits Bourgeois,[1] was not due to bad will or dishonesty. It was due in part, as might be guessed, to the pressure of other commitments, in part to an increasing number of illnesses, in part also to a perceptible decline in creative energy.

The reign of Gavault lasted from 1841 to 1844. He effected a steady, though not spectacular reduction in Balzac's massive debt. By 1844, for all his friendly services, his star was waning. His client suspected him of dilatoriness in dealing with Locquin, and also of too great affection for Sophie Koslowska, who took a severe view of Balzac's increasing ingratitude to her friend Sarah Guidoboni-Visconti. In 1845 another financial manager took charge, Auguste Fessart. He and Balzac hit upon the masterly idea of compounding for debts. If a creditor was himself in difficulties, or in despair at ever getting his money back, it was not impossible to persuade him to accept a percentage in final settlement. This device proved very useful for wiping out debts with tradesmen, although of course it depended on the creditor remaining convinced of Balzac's penury; that is why he grew so vexed when malicious tongues spread rumours of his affluence. By 1845, not only was Fessart hard at work, but also Balzac's and Mme Hanska's affairs were becoming intertwined. This, however, cut both ways, for while it put an even greater obligation on him to strive for solvency, it also gave him a new motive for squandering.

As for ill-health and incapacity for work, these two catastrophes came together. For years Balzac had had occasional trouble, mainly attacks of cerebral congestion brought on by overwork, and digestive upsets caused by the abuse of

---

[1] The former had been conceived in 1839, but Balzac never got beyond the preliminary pages, published in 1847. The latter was also conceived in 1839, partly set up in print in the spring of 1845, but never resumed. They were both completed and published after Balzac's death by Charles Rabou.

coffee and the lack of exercise. In November 1842 he suffered an attack of nervous prostration which kept him in bed for a fortnight, and his teeth were in bad condition. The Lagny effort of June–July 1843 wore him out. He was rewarded for it by a three-months' holiday in St. Petersburg. But while there he got sunstroke when attending a military review, and in November of that year he learned from Dr. Nacquart what was the cause of his many neuralgic headaches— he had contracted arachnitis, a form of chronic meningitis which may have dated back to his childhood, but which the sunstroke had aggravated. It was temporarily allayed by rest and treatment, but in 1844 the grinding toil began again, and this year he took no holidays. He was assailed in turn by toothache, neuralgia, nose-bleeding, nervous convulsions (the 'trismus' he mentions in *Petites Misères de la vie conjugale*), colic, six weeks of jaundice in March and April, and bronchitis in November. On November 3rd he wrote thus to Mme Hanska about his bronchitis:

Je n'ose pas me demander à moi-même si mes trois inflammations successives du foie, de la tête et des bronches n'ont pas une grande irritation intérieure pour cause.[1]

He still boasts of having an iron constitution, but it was beginning to crack. More relaxation in succeeding years (1845–7) buoyed him up at intervals and temporarily renewed his vigour and *joie de vivre*. But not only minor complaints—cholerina in 1846, eye-trouble and tonsillitis in 1847, and an almost regular succession of sprains from falls —were to come his way. Cardiac hypertrophy, the most dread disease of all, was in the offing. The symptoms appeared in 1847, and by the next year he knew what they meant. A doctor of medicine writing about Balzac has

[1] *E.*, ii, 450.

recently hazarded the opinion that acquired syphilis was the root of many of these chronic disorders.[1]

That a growing sense of fatigue and sterility should accompany these experiences is natural. From 1842 onwards, hours and days of vacancy of mind, not altogether unknown in earlier times, became frequent. In April 1842 he writes

> ... je ne me sens plus d'agilité dans la pensée, ni de rapidité dans la conception. Je ne vois plus de fraîcheur dans les images, ni de réflexions neuves dans la trame de mon œuvre.[2]

And two days later

> Je ne puis plus soutenir cette lutte tout seul, après quinze ans de constants travaux! Créer, toujours créer! Dieu n'a créé que pendant six jours.[3]

Complaints of utter tiredness, of inability to think or concentrate, of the inefficacy of his libations of coffee, of the need to take time off for amusement, are multiplied as the months roll on, and the cry for rest becomes more frequent and more desperate. Yet he still had periods of brilliant and powerful inspiration. In the intervals of woes and complaints he hammered out some of his best works. A wonderful recrudescence of imaginative energy resulted in *Les Parents pauvres* of 1846–7, and carried his reputation to a higher pitch than it had ever reached. The fact is that lateness with contracts, failing productivity, onsets of illness and inertia are all linked up, after 1841, with the peripeteias of the Hanska affair. When, in January 1842, Balzac learned that Ève was a widow, had he been able to guess that eight years would elapse before he was united to her, would he have gone on driving himself to death in order to get his work finished and his debts settled? Perhaps it is a pity that Ève

[1] Marcel Cazenove, *Le Drame de Balzac* (Delmas, 1950), pp. 206–10.
[2] *E.*, ii, 35–6, 27 April 1842.   [3] *E.*, ii, 37, 29 April 1842.

did not tear herself free of him, as at times she was minded to do, early in 1842. Balzac would probably never have worked off his debts, but he might have taken life more easily. As it turned out, Mme Hanska brought Balzac to such a lamentable condition that, when relations with her were strained, when the date of new meetings were uncertain from week to week and month to month, he lost all will to work. From 1845 onwards a new plaint is heard and often repeated: never will he be able to work again until they are married and living together.

In truth, after 1841 as never before, Balzac feels that his future is inseparably linked up with that of his 'belle Sarmate'.

Toutes mes actions, mes déterminations, mes pensées, n'ont de sens que par vous, vous en êtes le principe, le mobile secret, et je n'aurais plus de sens si vous veniez à me manquer.[1]

The swelling of his correspondence with her henceforward gives ample proof of this. The first volume of the *Lettres à l'Etrangère* (575 pages) covers nine years (1833–41). The second volume (471 pages) covers three years (1842–44). The third volume (377 pages) covers one and a half years (January 1845–20th August 1846). The fourth volume (379 pages) covers a period of just over twelve months (21st August 1846–3rd September 1847). These increases are caused by the habit Balzac acquired, and which he kept up except when work or illness prevented him, of writing her a daily letter and sending the result to her—his 'journal'—in periodic batches.

iii. Mme Hanska. 1842–3

Marriage with Ève meant the attainment of two life-long aims, worldly success and a satisfying love. In January 1842

[1] *E.*, ii, 59, 8 Aug. 1842.

he allowed himself to dream of a delightful future, when he and Ève would be living in Paris as man and wife,

> heureux, ayant un salon semblable à celui de Gérard, moi, dominant à la Chambre, et vous, une des reines de Paris, si difficile à fixer.[1]

Always the dormant political ambition! He fancied himself too as a member of the French Academy, though less for the glory it could give than for the financial perquisites it might bring.[2] But what bliss to enjoy all this in company with the gracious Countess: a Madame Firmiami made more captivating still by her foreign accent! How many times he repeated that he found in her all that his heart longed for:

> . . . l'amour, cette effusion des triples forces du cœur, de l'esprit et du corps, cet échange complet de la vie, cette cohésion parfaite de tous les points du cœur à tous les instants, cette divine admiration de l'un et de l'autre, ce culte de toutes les beautés, ce plaisir infini dans les moindres choses, cette satisfaction que donne un heureux choix et qui se reflète dans la jalousie d'autrui . . .[3]

But there were heavy clouds on the horizon. This fine lady belonged by race and upbringing to a social set from whose haughtiness he had everything to fear. His reluctance in 1844 and 1845 to see her at Dresden, which was crowded with Polish nobility, was due to consciousness of this. What relations would she have, as his wife, with his needy and querulous mother, the middle-class Laure, her husband and their two daughters? He must make it clear to Ève that she would be able to remain on politely distant terms with them once the inevitable formalities of meeting them were over. He did this, alas! from October 1842 onwards by systematic vilification of his mother in his letters to Ève. She was his worst enemy, 'l'auteur de tous mes maux,' one who had never been a true mother to him; one who was responsible

---

[1] *E.*, ii, 4, 11 Jan. 1842.
[2] *E.*, ii, 75; 14,000 francs per annum!   [3] *E.*, ii, 102, 20 Jan. 1843.

for his debts of 1828 (a monstrous assertion); one whose spite, calumny and intrigue, which charity might have wished to attribute to mental aberration, were born of sheer malevolence.[1] Laure's turn for disparagement was to come later, in 1846, for then he began to defame even that once beloved sister whose greatest crime, we may be sure, was that she had done her best to bring mother and son to reason in their dealings with one another.

How did Ève feel about all this? Perhaps the prospect of mingling with such unexciting people did not weigh too heavily among all the other considerations which might make her hesitate and postpone the date of marriage. This union, while it was impossible, had appeared romantically attractive; it seemed less so now that good faith made it almost an obligation. *Almost* an obligation. She was well aware of his past infidelities—with Mme Visconti and Caroline Marbouty in particular—and must have raised her eyebrows when he pleaded innocence as 'un pauvre amant, qui n'a pas eu une pensée à se reprocher dans sa longue et cruelle attente'.[2] Could she really have meant it when, at Vienna in 1835, she had given him *carte blanche* for the indulgence of his physical cravings, on condition that he formed no spiritual attachment with other women?[3] What would she have done if, in 1842, she had suspected that he was living on quasi-marital terms with Mme de Brugnol? She was not the woman to pass lightly even over peccadilloes, and Balzac's letters for the next three or four years were filled with protestations of cenobitic seclusion and continence. In making them he adhered to an established technique.

---

[1] *E.*, ii, 71, 17 Oct. 1842.   [2] *E.*, ii, 17–19.
[3] Ibid., 14–15. This seems to be implied in the words: 'N'ayez aucun attachement. Je ne veux que votre constance et votre coeur.' A letter of August 1846 (*E.*, iii, 363) shows that Ève actually suggested recourse to prostitutes to satisfy his needs.

Any woman who came under the searchlight of Ève's scrutiny automatically became old, ugly and malevolent as described by him. This includes the perennial Mme de Castries, with whom he still remained on passable terms, Mme Visconti who still untied her purse-strings on occasions, and many more purely social acquaintances. Mme d'Agoult became 'un effroyable *animal du désert*'.[1] Balzac's admiring Bettina, the Belgian Countess Ida de Bocarmé, is thus portrayed: '. . . à vingt-cinq ans cette pauvre femme est moins jeune que vous; elle met du rouge.'[2] Then there was Princess Belgiojoso. When he had first met her in 1833 she had been 'un chef-d'œuvre de beauté', second only to Ève herself.[3] Now she was 'prétentieuse à ne pas enfin être supportée deux heures'.[4] By 1844 she had become a hideous pervert, a man-stealer and a blue-stocking.[5] Between Ève and Honoré, an amusing note of double jealousy is sounded in the summer of that year. In 1842 he had given Franz Liszt a letter of introduction to Ève. Liszt visited her in St. Petersburg and did his best to captivate if not to seduce her. Ève virtuously dismissed him, but Balzac must have learned that she was not unflattered by Liszt's attention.[6] And so in 1844, while Ève was suspicious of Princess Belgiojoso, Balzac was venomous towards Liszt, whom he frequently met at the parties given by the Princess.[7]

Even actresses at the Odéon had had to lose their beauty to quiet Ève.[8] But such jealousy was after all a sign of possessive attachment. While fending off her blows, he must have derived some satisfaction from this thought. Unfortunately Ève had stronger motives for looking askance at the promised marriage. It is true that at times she looked forward to it. 'Attendre trois ans c'est la mort!' she wrote in November

[1] *E.*, ii, 160, 16 May 1843.   [2] *E.*, ii, 132, 31 March 1843.
[3] *L. F.*, 154.   [4] *E.*, ii, 160.   [5] *E.*, ii, 342, 417.
[6] Korwin-Piotrowska, pp. 312–20.   [7] *E.*, ii, 371.   [8] *E.*, ii, 26–7.

1842,[1] when Balzac, in pessimistic mood, suggested it would take that time to clear up her affairs and his commitments. But her relatives were keenly opposed to her marriage with an adventurer whose debts—so Aunt Rosalie insinuated—were mainly gambling ones, and who was deeply in love with her fortune. Her daughter Anna, now of marriageable age, raised another problem. Mother and daughter were devoted to each other. In April 1844 Balzac wrote of Anna: 'son plus beau moment, comme femme, sera entre dix-huit et vingt-trois ans; plus tard, elle grossira, deviendra hommasse. Cet arrêt est écrit dans son nez.'[2] If Ève passed this on to Anna, it is no wonder the latter was not as yet very fond of her prospective step-father. He, naturally, wanted to see her paired off quickly with a rich husband, and at this prospect Ève protested: 'Si ma pauvre enfant m'était ôtée, je mourrais.'[3] A still graver obstacle existed: a rich, aged, miserly cousin of the late M. Hanski whose fortune was destined for Anna. To prevent the misalliance, this family despot, whom Balzac dubbed 'Uncle Tamerlane', challenged the validity of Ève's marriage-contract of 1819, whereby she, on M. Hanski's demise, was to enjoy the usufruct of his vast estates. The court at Kiew upheld his point of view. Ève appealed against the decision, and so incurred a long and expensive law-suit. It took her in August 1842 to St. Petersburg, where she remained until May 1844, having at last won her appeal. While the case was undecided there could be no question of a second marriage.

For eighteen months then after Hanski's death, until he at last met Ève again, Balzac lived in a turmoil of emotions: worry over his work, his debts, his health; surges of anguish, tenderness, passion and despondency; fears over Ève's recriminations and tergiversations. Once, in February 1842,

[1] *E.*, ii, 82.   [2] *E.*, ii, 355.   [3] *E.*, ii, 14.

she had gone so far as to tell him: 'Vous êtes libre!' But through it all there was sufficient warmth in her letters, despite her caprices and revulsions of feeling, to keep hope alive. In happier moments (as in July 1842), he discussed ways and means for their setting up as a married couple in France: a house in Paris, with Les Jardies, not yet finally discarded, or a château in the country, for summer residence. His budgetary discussion on that occasion stirred him to self-admiration, but he made Souverain his trumpeter: 'Il sait mieux calculer que Rothschild!'[1] When long delays seemed unavoidable, he lamented over his lot: 'Aussi ne demandé-je à Dieu que la certitude. Cette certitude me ferait tout sup-porter.'[2] At such times he cast about him for any assurance or consolation. He even hankered after a second consultation with the fortune-teller Balthazar. At the 1841 consultation Balthazar had divined the tenacity of Balzac's love. 'Vous n'avez jamais aimé *qu'elle*, et *vous ne pouvez aimer qu'elle, vous n'aimerez plus personne. C'est physique.*'[3] He had promised a happy consummation, but had not told him when it was to be. In 1843 this prophet was in gaol for abor-tionism.

At last the sky cleared. In the summer of 1843, putting the ordeal of Lagny behind him, Balzac booked his sea-passage to St. Petersburg, where Ève awaited him. Buisson was called upon for sartorial ministrations, and off Balzac went 'brand-new, like a bride'. He arrived on the 29th July, with over two months of happiness in front of him and the hope of marriage at the end of it. Each of the pair felt anxious about the impression each would make. Had the years taken too great toll of her beauty or of his virile charm? Misgivings fell from them when they met. Balzac in person, an impetuous and masterful lover, was vastly

[1] *E.*, ii, 52.   [2] *E.*, ii, 91.   [3] *E.*, ii, 146; 24 April 1843.

different from the harassed toiler writing across 1,500 miles of space. Ève was reconquered.

iv. St. Petersburg and after. 1843–5

Of Balzac's sojourn in St. Petersburg little is known. He had toyed with the idea of settling there, of winning Imperial favour, of starting a literary and dramatic school. He thought of earning shelter in Russia by refuting the Marquis de Custine's *La Russie en 1839*. He read Bettina von Arnim's account of her correspondence with Goethe—a 'pen-friendship' on which he frowned—and wrote a criticism of it. That, and his failure to penetrate into the aristocratic society of the capital, matters little. The love between him and Ève, though they were now both middle-aged, was entering upon a new phase.

Pétersbourg? Le salon bleu de la Néva! C'est la première initiation de mon minou, c'est sa première éducation. Quelle union de deux mois, sans une note fausse, si ce n'est la querelle du chapeau et celle à propos de la dépense d'une cuisinière.[1]

They were both strongly sensual as well as emotional. As M. Billy puts it, 'Cette grosse femme brune et ce gros homme brun se plaisaient beaucoup.' They took to childish endearments, called one another 'loup' and 'louloup', and in subsequent letters were not shy about making allusions, by means of erotic terms and symbols, to the physical satisfactions they enjoyed together. At least Balzac was not shy about it, and therefore Ève must have approved. While his health lasted he maintained this hold on her, and the momentum gained while they were together was sufficient to carry them over the many voids and chasms which still separated them from legal union. Certainly Balzac's ardour was more sustained, and more consuming than that of Ève,

[1] *E.*, iii, 149; 12 Dec. 1845.

who remained as subject as ever to scruples and repentances,
to onsets of pride, anger, mistrust, and lassitude. With him
love had become an obsession. The desire to possess her
securely, intensified by the prospect of ease and rest, became
akin to the monomanias portrayed in his novels: Grandet's
greed, Goriot's paternal frenzy, Bette Fischer's rancour,
Baron Hulot's lust.

. . . Je fais pour mon Ève toutes les folies qu'un Hulot fait pour une
Marneffe; je te donnerais mon sang, mon honneur, ma vie! . . .[1] Oh!
minette, je baise tes jolies paupières, je savoure ton bon col, à cet
endroit qui est comme le nid des baisers, et je tiens tes pattes de taupe
dans mes mains, et je sens le parfum qui rend fou, et je te dis, en
jouissant par la pensée de ces mille trésors, dont un seul suffirait à
l'orgueil d'une femme bête: 'O *louloup*, ô mon Èvelette, mon âme
aime encore plus ton âme, et mon regret est de ne pas pouvoir
caresser cette âme, la saisir, m'en emparer, la posséder, comme j'ai
ton front, ne fût-ce que pour devenir meilleur en participant à toi, à
ton essence si éthérée, si parfaite.'[2]
. . . Ah, il n'y a pas de bonheur sans toi! Je suis amoureux comme un
fou; je suis depuis hier que je me repose, en face de cette idée: 'la voir!'
J'ai besoin de toi comme on a faim. C'est brutal . . .[3]

At St. Petersburg, it seems, the understanding was reached
that marriage should take place once the obstacles to it were
removed on either side; that is to say, when the question of
Ève's inheritance was settled and her daughter married,
and when Balzac had wiped out his debts. In October Balzac
set off homewards by the overland route, with some of Ève's
money in his pocket, and full of noble resolutions about
economy—but also intent on preparing a home for his beloved and furnishing it in style. The second purpose threatened to cancel out the first. Before long Ève was frowning
over his propensity to waste money on antique furniture,
pictures and ornaments. It was indeed about this time that

[1] *E.*, iv, 165, 12 Dec. 1846.
[2] *E.*, iii, 123–4, 13 Nov. 1845.   [3] *E.*, iii, 336, 28 July 1846.

his 'bric-à-bracomania', already chronic, became a passion.
A classic instance is the case of the 'Florentine furniture',
the *bahuts* which he bought in December 1843 for 1,400
francs. He was convinced that these articles, a writing-desk
and chest of drawers in ebony, inlaid with mother-of-pearl,
had been made at the order of Marie de Medici, consort of
Henri IV, and that the writing-desk had passed on to the
Concini, her favourites. 'Quand on pense qu'Henri IV a
posé souvent ses mains sur cette commode!'

He was delighted with his purchase. He would keep the
secrétaire and sell the commode to the King for the Som-
merard Museum, for 3,000 francs: a clear profit of 1,600
francs! The following month he was longing to buy a pair of
Dresden vases when Ève's chilling comment on the purchase of the *bahuts* arrived: 'Si vous ne savez pas résister à la
commode d'Henri IV, vous ne résisterez à rien, à aucune
passion.'[1] The shaft went home, and for a long time henceforward it was a question of selling, not one, but both of the
articles: to the King, to the Queen, to an English Duke, to
Sir Robert Peel, for 20,000 francs, for 60,000 francs, for
£3,000; and two years later to the King of Holland, for
70,000 francs. He never managed to get rid of either. Such
purchases as this were frequent; he was always finding bar-
gains. Ève herself was not immune from the weakness
of supposing that antique-dealers do not know the worth of
what they are selling. Yet for all his gullibility and excess of
enthusiasm, Balzac had some flair as a collector, though less
than that which he attributed to the hero of his 1847 novel,
Le cousin Pons. By that year he had accumulated a houseful
of antiques for the embellishment of his and Ève's future
home. It was the cost of all these articles that worried
her.

[1] *E.*, ii, 280, 23 Jan. 1844.

At the New Year of 1844 she was still at St. Petersburg
with Anna. When in February he learned that she had won
her law-suit, Balzac's jubilation expressed itself in one of his
most lyrical love-letters. There were still legal formalities to
deal with, and the Hanski couple did not return to Wierzchownia until June. In the meanwhile Balzac was having a
bad time—ill-health, over-work, impatience. In June he
nursed the hope of spending two years among the corn-fields
of Wierzchownia, but when Ève arrived home this was
found to be impossible. She had been fleeced in her absence,
her estates were all in disorder, and although 'Uncle Tamerlane' was now in a more amiable frame of mind, her
situation was still dubious. Balzac himself was disturbed by
the rumour that the Russian Government was threatening
to confiscate the property of all Polish landowners who refused to embrace the Orthodox faith. Anna's future had still
to be decided, and the Tsar's consent had to be obtained for
marriage with a foreigner.

And so, perforce, Balzac still 'sigh'd his soul toward the
Grecian tents' until the summer of 1845. He had now, as
some slight consolation, the original Daffinger miniature of
Ève, as well as other lovers' relics, to fondle. Until then he
had had only a copy. 'Ma sœur,' he wrote, 'a dit en voyant
le Daffinger que c'était impossible qu'une femme fût aussi
jolie que cela.'

A lover's infatuation? How beautiful in fact was Ève? If
we may judge by this same miniature, painted at Vienna
when she was 33, she was reasonably so. Black ringlets, a
face more oval than round, an imposingly broad forehead, a
well-chiselled nose, neat mouth, tight lips; the chin grace-
fully curved but obstinate. Physiognomists may read into
her face the mingled sensuality and religious emotionalism
we know she possessed. But what stands out is an impression

of self-importance and pettishness; and the promise of a
fuming temper.[1]

By 1844 she was filling out, as Balzac's frequent endearments—*ma grasse Ève*—prove. We must turn for ocular
evidence to a later portrait. Gigoux painted her in half-
profile when she was 52. By now she has run to fat, and the
contours of the cheeks have lost their firmness. The chin is
almost rounded into a ball, but is quite obtrusive. The lips
are fuller and more sensual, with a hint of cruelty in them.
The glance of the eyes is firm, perhaps softened by sadness
or regret. The total impression is displeasing; to the spon-
taneous imperiousness of 1835 is added the suggestion of a
more settled self-centredness.[2]

In 1932 a Polish sculptor, Francis Black, did a bust of her
in marble: a reconstruction based on 'original documents
and in particular the Daffinger miniature'. Being synthetic
it can scarcely be faithful, but in spite of the strong, almost
harshly sullen set of the mouth, it is more pleasing than the
portraits. The face is solemn, the mood almost morose. But
it suggests sincerity as well as purposefulness, and a power
to charm should the features relax into a smile. It gives the
woman rather than the countess.[3]

With half a continent between them Balzac experienced
more of the countess than the woman.

The last months of 1843 and the whole of 1844 find him
engaged in many activities: as usual correcting his proof-
sheets for the 'Comédie Humaine'; writing such works as
Modeste Mignon on a theme recently supplied by Ève herself, that of a love-match born, like theirs, of a romantic
correspondence; continuing *Splendeurs et misères des courti-*

[1] See Pl. xxxiii in P. Abraham, *Balzac*, 1929.
[2] See the reproduction in M. Bouteron, *La véritable Image de Mme
Hanska* (Lapina, 1929), p. 2.
[3] See Korwin-Piotrowska, *op. cit.*, frontispiece.

sanes, begun in 1838, and *l'Envers de l'histoire contemporaine*, begun in 1842; and providing a third part and a
happy conclusion for *Béatrix*; groaning over *Les petits Bourgeois* and *Les Paysans*; taking soundings for his prospects
of admission to the French Academy, and mourning, in
January 1844, the death of Charles Nodier who might have
helped him to get elected in spite of the Academicians' reluctance to admit a chronic debtor to their Olympian confraternity; completing the sittings for his bust by David,
which a technical objection prevented from being shown in
the Salon of 1844; trying to get his shiftless brother Henri a
better post in the Île-Bourbon, and staving off importunate
demands of money from his mother; keeping a fair number
of social engagements, with the Girardins, Victor Hugo,
George Sand, Princess Belgiojoso, Baron Rothschild and the
Chlendowskis.

This much in the face of the world at large. But also, with
his gaze ardently turned towards Wierzchownia, and then
towards Dresden whither Ève and Anna moved at the end
of November 1844, he was excusing himself for rash purchases, justifying his tireless searches for a house or building-
site in or outside Paris, since the house in the Rue Basse was
now noisy, crowded with workmen's families and swarming
with children. Les Jardies was at last paid for but soon to be
finally, genuinely sold. It no longer suited his plans. He was
trying to persuade Ève to buy a plot or even five plots of land
on the Monceaux gardens estate which the King was selling
off. 'Ceci, mon *louloup*, n'est pas *spéculer*, c'est *placer*.'[1] It is
comic to see him showering advice on Ève as to health,
hygiene and cosmetics, as well as the management of her
affairs and the placing of her monies; and urging her to sup-
press all needless luxury, to save up so as to make herself and

[1] *E.*, iii, 54.

Anna (and Balzac) independent of inconvenient Imperial *ukases*. 'Faites-vous avare.'[1] He reminds her, when the occasion seems to require it, that in marrying him she will not be flinging herself away:

En 1846, nous aurons une des plus délicieuses maisons de Paris, je n'aurai plus un sou de dettes. . . . Si je n'épouse pas, selon votre mot, une pauvresse, vous n'épouserez pas non plus un pauvre.[2]

One of the commissions Ève had assigned to him before he left St. Petersburg was to watch over the affairs of Anna's former governess, the spinster from Neuchâtel, Henriette Borel, familiarly known as 'Lirette'. Once Anna was off her hands this erstwhile Protestant was anxious to become a nun. Balzac and Mme de Brugnol welcomed her on her arrival at Paris in June 1844, and gave her hospitality until the clerics concerned had decided what order she should enter. Rothschild, with whom henceforth, as Ève's Paris banker, Balzac had much to do, looked after the business-side of the affair, arranged with the convent about her dowry, and invested the rest of her savings as a safeguard for the future. To be a cicerone of would-be postulants was a new rôle for Balzac. In his letters to Ève he narrates the story of the naïve Lirette in Paris until and after her taking of the veil, as Sœur Marie-Dominique, at the Convent of the Visitation on the 2nd of December 1845. His mental reactions are worth noting: stupefaction at the sight of a woman all agog to quit the world, not unmingled with apprehension, for in moments of perplexity Ève herself was still liable to dally with the idea; contempt tinged with indignation at the thought of Lirette wishing to surrender more money than she need; anger at her impatience to put the world, and even her friends, behind her and to

---

[1] *E.*, ii, 369, 3 June, 1844.   [2] *E.*, ii, 464, 16 Dec., 1844.

plunge into conventual routine; aesthetic and emotional curiosity about the ceremony itself, which he found august and imposing; and finally disgust, when he paid her a visit in November 1846, at the 'égoïsme' she displayed in only allotting him five minutes in the parlour when it had taken him an hour to get to her convent.

In the autumn of 1844, the ingenuous, affectionate and susceptible Anna met a young Polish count of considerable wealth, or prospects of wealth: George Mniszech, a mild and pleasant young man who had a talent for drawing and a passion for entomology. They liked each other, and when mother and daughter left for Dresden, George went with them on a period of probation. It was in vain that Balzac opposed the match, simply on the grounds that, because of the Tsar's hostility to Poles, it was imprudent for Anna to marry one. They became engaged. With Ève at Dresden, and so much nearer to Paris, Balzac's impatience at long separation increased. He had had a difficult year, and, in the early months of 1845, complained repeatedly about the effect that Ève's changes of plan and alterations of moods were having on him:

> J'ai été tenaillé, torturé comme jamais je ne l'ai été. C'est un triple martyre, celui du cœur, celui de la tête, celui des affaires.[1]

He had wanted her to come nearer than Dresden, chiefly because he knew that in that city were congregated Ève's compatriots and relations—especially her soured old kinswoman Caroline Galitzin—who hoped to prevent her marriage with the Frenchman. Ève too realized that Dresden was not the best place for them to meet. But the Dresden clique had reawakened old doubts in her mind as to whether their love was really strong enough to warrant marriage. The perplexity was doubtless genuine, for she was an im-

---

[1] *E.*, iii, 17; 15 Feb. 1845.

pressionable and temperamental woman. She felt they must meet again for it to be resolved. Anxious as he was to go, Balzac had too many commitments to rush away at a moment's notice. Then in April a summons arrived: *Je voudrais te voir.* On the 24th of April Balzac learned that he had been awarded the Cross of the Legion of Honour. He was too excited to care much about that. By May, he was in Dresden.

v. Dresden and after. 1845–7

It is a point in Ève's favour that when he was with her he was happy in the main. He was now to be with her for nearly four months and to enjoy further reunions at not very long intervals—much to the detriment of his programme of work. Dresden was uncongenial, and the four moved on to Hombourg, Cannstadt, Karlsruhe. They became quite a harmonious quartet. In playful affection they adopted sobriquets from the popular farce of *Les Saltimbanques.* Ève was Atala, Anna was Zéphyrine, George was Gringalet. Balzac was the hero of the piece: Bilboquet. He had no difficulty in winning the friendship of the engaged couple.

Ève was now in a mood for prolonged enjoyment, and charmingly disposed to her 'amant-mari', her 'Noré louloup'. He made preparations for mother and daughter to visit Paris while George remained in Germany. A brief stay at Strasbourg brought great joy to Balzac: he and Ève went one day to a monastery chapel and there joined hands in mystic union. He looked upon this henceforward as equivalent to marriage in God's eyes. In any case it was a solemn promise: 'la certitude d'un mutuel bonheur'.

Then he escorted 'Mme et Mlle Surville' to Paris for a day or two. A trip in the country followed: Fontainebleau,

Orléans, Bourges (Frapesle was near at hand, but Zulma was not honoured with a call), Tours, Blois. Back to Paris again, and then a tour through Belgium and Holland. Sweet companionship! They went round antique-shops together and bought bric-à-brac. As she paid the piper, Ève preferred to call the tune. Balzac tried to call it at Rotterdam over a wardrobe: there were sharp exchanges, but the quarrel blew over. Back to Brussels, where George rejoined them. Then Balzac returned to Paris, and tried to do three weeks' work. Ève went to Baden to take the waters. At the end of September he joined her there for a week: another honeymoon! Back in Paris, he was occupied with publishers' contracts. Then came another trip. He picked up the trio at Châlons-sur-Saône and escorted them to Toulon, and thence by boat to Naples. He left them there to winter in Italy, and returned by way of Marseilles, where he spent several days in the company of his friend Méry, the Marseillais poet, dramatist and novelist. An antique-dealer, Lazard, put much temptation in his way at Marseilles, and he yielded to it.

The 18th of November saw him in Paris once again, still in a state of partial euphoria, though he had a few embarrassing accusations to ward off. One of Ève's sisters, Aline Moniusko, all envy and malice, but the mother of two fair daughters, had been making mischief. So had the 'infamous spy', Dr Koreff, of magnetic memory; so had Balzac's Bettina, the 'infamous woman' Ida de Bocarmé. How should the now ageing Balzac be an 'amateur de chair fraîche' (Aline's expression) when his sole fear is that he is not young enough for Ève? What matter if the tailor Buisson (and later Hubert, the mason he had employed at Les Jardies) are deaf to the voice of the charmer Fessart and stand out for the full payment of debt? What matter if Balzac has another of his many falls and tears a muscle? In

March 1846 he is back at Marseilles, where he is fêted and
banqueted by Méry and the admiring youth of the town.
Then to Rome. Sight-seeing with Ève. Easter celebrations.
Kissing the Pope's slipper. More bargain-hunting with Ève,
this time in search of Old Masters. A blissful return together
from Rome: Genoa, Geneva, Les Grisons, Bâle and Heidel-
burg. At Soleure, in Switzerland, a wonderful hope dawns.
Is Ève with child? He will learn for certain that she is, on
the 2nd of June, when back in Paris. 'Les louloups seront une
tribu.' His sex is chosen in advance, and his name: Victor-
Honoré. Surely Noré is now within a stone's throw of
Paradise?

The child must be born in wedlock. But marriage is not
so easy for a wandering Russian widow. There are formal difficulties. The lovers meet again at Maintz in early
September. Where and when shall the wedding be? At a
frontier town of France, with the connivance of the local
prefect and a docile mayor? At Passy, from a quiet hotel?
This is feasible once Ève has found the necessary certificates.
Strange to say, she is not fanatical about the birth in wedlock. She would rather make sure that her affairs at Wierzchownia are in good order. At any rate both are agreed it is
better to get Anna and George settled, particularly since the
death of George's father. The young couple are married at
Wiesbaden in October. Balzac is a witness, and spreads the
news, in the French newspapers, of the wedding of 'one of
the richest heiresses in the Russian Empire'. By now he is
back in Paris, with four more months of separation in front
of him.

Victor-Honoré had to be housed as well as legitimized.
How confusing to a reader of the *Lettres* is the succession
of residences that Noré proposed to his Evelina during the
periods of separation! In December 1845 his sister Laure had

put him on the track of a house, with ugly frontage, three floors and an ice-chamber beneath, which he thought might suit them: not far east of L'Étoile, 14 Rue Fortunée (now Rue Balzac), the annexe of a large mansion built in 1781 by the financier Beaujon, 'La Folie Beaujon'. It is the second 'Folie Balzac', his final abode in Paris after May 1847: but it is more kindly referred to as the 'Maison Balzac'. On this, for three and a half years to come, he was to squander love, dreams, care and money (mostly Ève's) to make it a fitting shrine for his divinity. He contracted to buy it at the end of September 1846 without waiting for Ève's disapproval. The price was 50,000 francs. In 1882 it was sold again for 500,000 francs—but only for demolition.

After Wiesbaden Ève became annoyed with him once more. Since Dresden they had had a financial account in common. She had entrusted him with capital, the *trésor louloup*. In due course it rose to the handsome sum of 130,000 francs, and was intended for the purchase of a house and furniture, and for the extinction of some of his debts. With such sums in his hands, he had grown rash. 'Ne t'épouvante pas de mes acquisitions. . . . Repose-toi sur mon énorme bon sens.'[1] He had invested part of it, through Rothschild, in shares of the newly-founded Chemin de Fer du Nord, which Rothschild had helped to launch. He hoped to make an easy fortune by their rise in value. They dropped and dropped, and continued to do so for several years. They were not fully paid-up to begin with, and there were frequent calls by the company on the shareholders. To make matters worse, Noré began to raise loans on the security of the shares, notably from the Viscontis. By July 1847 he had mortgaged them to the amount of 50,000 francs, and their sale-value had fallen to 70,000. In November 1846, vexed

[1] *E.*, iii, 309, 11 July 1846.

and alarmed, Ève refused to endorse his ventures any further. 'Arrange-toi comme tu pourras avec les Rothschild; ne compte sur moi pour rien.'

But he still hoped to get her to Paris for the birth of Victor-Honoré, in spite of the discomfort of travel for a pregnant woman.

> . . . Ne t'inquiète pas du voyage; tu le feras en parfaite santé, car je te magnétiserai depuis Leipsick jusqu'à Paris, et tu n'auras pas une douleur, je te le promets. Je suis en ce moment, par suite de mes travaux et de ma chasteté, d'une énorme puissance magnétique. . . .[1]

Unluckily for him, she soon ceased to be pregnant. On December 1st he learned that there had been a miscarriage. She did not even favour his impulse to rush to Dresden to see her and console her. A hurried wedding was no longer necessary.

> Il est dit que ma vie sera un long assassinat! . . . Attendre encore! Attendre, lorsque quarante-sept ans sont sonnés, lorsque tant d'efforts, tant d'amour ont épuisé, rassuré mon pauvre être, tour à tour![2]

What was to happen now? Ève was burning to get back to Wierzchownia, and talking of postponing the marriage until October 1847. Not even his prophecy of a European conflagration (for once he praised Louis-Philippe for having made France strong and a sure haven of refuge) could persuade her to doff her Russian nationality and settle in France before the storm broke.

So the end of 1846 found Balzac in deep depression. It had been a year of much elation, with intervals of despondency, much achievement (above all *La cousine Bette* and the final touches to the long-standing *Petites Misères de la vie conjugale*), and desultory sociability. Even from the guarded and garbled accounts given in the *Lettres*, we may perceive that, when away from Ève in Paris, he was no re-

[1] *E.*, iv, 120, 17 Nov. 1846.   [2] *E.*, iv, 137, 138, 1 Dec. 1846.

cluse. Friendship with Mme de Castries was still flickering. Delphine de Girardin was still attentive, and coaxed him to her parties to meet distinguished foreigners, including Cobden, and prominent figures of the Paris political world. Is it worth while recording also that in early 1846 he had carried indirect epistolary abuse of his mother to the extremest pitch? or that she did something to earn this abuse in June by overstating his debt to her? or, by way of light relief, that in this year a ship-builder from Le Havre named a boat after Balzac? It was a whaler.

In 1847 there were new ups and downs in his relations with Ève. Noré went on with his purchases: Ève must have for instance a bed-chamber furnished with Buhl, and a *salon en marqueterie*. He went on with his calculations of debts, investments, future liabilities and future solvency, turning and pacing like a captive beast within the iron bars of his financial cage. And she went on alternating cold douches with tender reminiscences. His pleas and excuses are at once pathetic and absurd.

Je n'ai pas le moindre goût au bric-à-brac; j'achète chez les marchands de curiosités de belles choses à cinquante pour cent moins que si j'en faisais faire de laides neuves, car le beau est hors de prix à faire fabriquer.[1]

. . . Oh! petit Évelin, ô cher camarade, ô ma Linette, mon Évelette, ma petite fille, vous serez bien furieuse contre vous-même un jour, de voir que vous vous êtes laissée aller à penser comme le bête de public sur votre Noré, que votre Noré est joueur, libertin, dissipateur; quand vous trouverez qu'il a travaillé nuit et jour, qu'il ne touche pas une carte, qu'il ne pense qu'à vous, qu'il est économe, qu'il a une maison admirablement meublée et montée [the 'maison Balzac'], et qu'il ne doit pas un sou et qu'il a conservé notre *trésor-louloup*, que vous l'avez grondé inutilement et qu'il a tout fait pour le mieux.[2]

. . . O vanité! dira la sage Évelinette. Et quand tu verras cela, tu diras: 'Comment, mon Noré, ça n'a coûté que cela [55,000 francs,

[1] *E.*, iv, 209, 3 Jan. 1847.   [2] *E.*, iv, 215, 8 Jan. 1847.

according to his own modest figures, for altering and furnishing the house; but in a letter to his sister of January 1849 he was to put the total cost at 400,000 francs]? Oh! comme tu as bien fait, comme nous serons heureux là![1]

And when he feared that such a benediction would never fall on his ears, that the hope of life together in Paris would never be realized, his imagination took him in flight to the steppes of the Ukraine. He soothed his weariness with the hope of rest and dreamful ease at Wierzchownia, as a naturalized Russian, a 'Bilboquetinski' who should win such repose as a propagandist for Imperial absolutism might earn from a suspicious Tsar.

Je n'écrirais plus . . . Je vivrais en rêveur, et le plus heureux des hommes du monde, le chien, le moujick de mon loup, toujours près de toi, ne te quittant pas.[2]

In the early spring of 1847 Balzac found himself yet again on the crest of the wave. He had not seen Ève since Wiesbaden. She had gone to Dresden, then to Frankfort. On the 10th of February she allowed him to bring her to Paris, and until the beginning of May they lived together in an apartment at Passy. It was an incognito visit, but she held herself free to go with him to the Opera, to theatres, to concerts, to meet with some of his friends, to savour as much of the exhilaration of literary Paris as he could offer to her in such circumstances; also to keep an eye on structural and furnishing operations at the house in the Rue Fortunée, to which, after much demur, she was now resigned. Then they parted again. She returned by slow stages to Wierzchownia for the purpose of settling her estates on Anna in return for a life-annuity, for this turned out to be the only means whereby she could be free to marry a foreigner without being denuded of worldly goods. While she was with him in Paris

[1] *E.*, iv, 236, 21 Jan. 1847.　　[2] *E.*, iv, 219, 10 Jan. 1847.

Balzac had put on what was virtually his last spurt in novel-writing: *Le cousin Pons*, *La dernière incarnation de Vautrin*, and the first and only authentic part of *Le Député d'Arcis*.

More trouble cropped up once he was back in Paris, now installed at the 'Maison Balzac'—uncomfortably, for the workmen were still in. He was still spending much money on it, in order to convert it into the 'vraie bijoutière' he wished it to be. In July 1845 Ève's suspicious glance had fallen on Mme de Brugnol. She had demanded her dismissal. Now Balzac's housekeeper-mistress had been extremely useful to him. She had been more of a business-agent than a housekeeper, a bulwark against creditors, a signer of bills, and a *prête-nom* for transactions in which he did not want his own name to appear. She was the nominal lessee for the house at Passy, and he wanted her to sign the contract for a new house when he found it. And so, although he gave her notice in July 1845, she remained with him for nearly two years more. He still needed her, if only in preparing for the installation of her rival and successor. And in common decency he had to make some provision for her future, to repay what he owed her, to give her a viaticum of, say, 7,500 francs, to persuade the Ministry to allot her a tobacco-shop or a stamp-office, or to find her a husband.

His letters to Ève contain a running commentary on the efforts he made to achieve these aims. And of course he felt himself obliged to blacken her character in order to mollify Ève. She had for long been nicknamed 'La Montagnarde': a tribute to her staunch fidelity to his interests, similar to the fanatical adherence that the party of the 'Montagne' had maintained in 1792–3 to Revolutionary principles? She now became 'la Mégère', 'la donzelle', or, more frequently, 'la Chouette', in punning reference to Elshoëcht, the wood-carver whom, in the course of 1846, she was hoping to marry.

When Balzac left the Passy house in February 1847 she was finally dismissed.

She had been ungratefully treated. She took her revenge. After Ève left Paris in May 1847 Balzac discovered that Mme de Brugnol had purloined a number of Ève's letters to himself, compromising ones which contained allusions to Victor-Honoré and possibly worse. She proceeded to hold him to ransom for them, while at the same time she jeopardized his position with his creditors by circulating rumours of his forthcoming marriage with a wealthy woman. Balzac was panic-stricken, and divulged all this to Ève in such a way as to make her panic-stricken too. He threatened Mme de Brugnol with legal proceedings, and she in her turn grew alarmed. But Balzac was advised to come to terms with her and pay her 5,000 francs for the letters—in addition to the money which he genuinely owed her. After much turmoil, this course was agreed upon.

In 1848 Mme de Brugnol fell on her feet without Balzac's direct aid. With such sums as she managed to extract from him—he was not quit of her as regards debt until late 1849 —she bought herself a profitable bronze-merchant's shop and a satisfactory husband. Though her methods were questionable, she probably deserved this happy settlement.

In the summer of 1847 this business was far from being settled, and a cold wind was blowing again from Wierzchownia, whither Ève had returned in June. In addition to a host of other subjects for querulous complaint, came physical ills. Foremost among them was the chronic arachnitis. It was followed by symptoms of heart-disease, of which a fellow-author, Frédéric Soulié, was even then dying: a grim portent of things to come, although he was inclined to attribute the pains he felt to a stomach-upset caused by coffee. Perhaps it was concern for his health, rising triumphant over her irritation at his financial incorrigibility and the wrath inspired by the Brugnol blackmail, that induced Ève to consent in August to his visiting Wierzchownia. Such was his resilience that he immediately felt himself to be on top of fortune's wheel again. But he made his will before he left: everything to Ève, debts and all, provided she make provision for his mother; or, if she refused, assets and debts to his mother, with incidental bequests to Ève and others. He was also constrained by Ève to destroy all the letters he had had from her: a heart-breaking holocaust.

vi. Wierzchownia and after. 1847–8

For one who, on the 17th of August, was talking of ending his miseries with digitalis, Balzac made a surprisingly vigorous dash across Europe: to Cologne, Hanover, Berlin, Breslaw, Cracow, mostly over the primitive railways of the time; thence across Galicia by mail-coach. At Radziwilloff an enlightened frontier official put a swift vehicle, a *kitbitka*, at his disposal, with a Cossack to drive it. After a change of vehicle at Berditcheff, Wierzchownia was reached on the 13th of September. Eager, gay, impatient, inexhaustible, Balzac had forced the pace and tired out the Cossack.

Experiences during this journey are vivaciously described in the extant fragment of the 'Lettre sur Kiew' which he started writing at Wierzchownia for the *Journal des Débats*, but which remained unfinished because, when he went to Kiew in November, the prevalence of cholera prevented him from collecting material. He was impressed with the size and fertility of Ukraine, and enchanted with the palatial residence of the Hanskis. He found himself in the heart of an immense feudal estate of 50,000 acres, cultivated (in so far as cultivation of such an area was possible) by over 3,000 male serfs. He waxed enthusiastic over their happy lot, marred only by their addiction to vodka. The Wierzchownia community was self-sufficing. It had its own staple industries, a Roman Catholic chapel and a hospital. Its cloth-factory provided him with a warm overcoat lined with Siberian silver fox-skins. The mansion itself was an odd mixture of luxury and discomfort: bare walls, straw for fuel, and one single Carcel lamp. The late M. Hanski had had his own orchestra; it had now diminished to one violin.

It is typical of Balzac that almost as soon as he arrived he conceived a grandiose scheme for the further enrichment of his hosts, himself and the Survilles: the sale of timber for railway-sleepers in France, to be cut from the forests of Wisniowicz, the Mniszech estates. He unfolded it in detail in a letter to Laure, only to discover before receiving her reply that the cost of transport would be prohibitive. He spent most of his time more profitably. As his correspondence was now reduced to letters to his mother and sister, and as he only told them what he thought fit that they should know, information is lacking about the reception he received from Ève and her family. But reading between the lines we may assume that it was warm and cordial. With his old cheerfulness and vivacity restored they must have found him a naïvely enthusiastic visitor and an entertaining guest. Apart from a heavy cold, his health seems to have given no trouble. He had a pleasant suite of rooms in which he spent the day-time working: sketching out the 'Lettre sur Kiew', writing most of *L'Initié* (the last part of *L'Envers de l'histoire contemporaine*), and beginning other works. Though he received occasional visits from his hosts, he only came out of his shell at dinner-time. He hoped to stay there until the following April, but his eternal affairs (chiefly another call on the Nord shareholders) summoned him back

to Paris in the middle of February. He brought some more
of Ève's money with him.

Wierzchownia had restored his courage and equanimity,
but troubles were in store. He discovered that on the 13th of
February *Le Siècle* had published a sarcastic article about his
journey to Russia and slandered Ève and the Rzewuskis.
Then the Revolution of February broke out: street fighting,
barricades, fraternization of the National Guard with the
populace, the abdication of Louis-Philippe, the proclamation
of the Republic, the sack of the Tuileries. Balzac shared in
the general excitement, joined the mob which sacked the
Tuileries, and came away with some historical souvenirs—
fragments of drapery from the throne, and exercise-books
belonging to the dispossessed princes. But he was still no
republican, although momentarily flattered by the invi-
tation of one of the revolutionary clubs to stand for the
Constituent Assembly. He accurately foresaw the shape of
things to come: weak government, riots and massacres, and
the arrival of a dictator. Moreover the Revolution and the
uncertainty it caused, in Europe as well as in France, promised ill for the success of his plans: making more money
by writing, salvaging his investments which were suffering
from the general slump, and achieving the marriage which
Ève had refused to contemplate until she could be sure that
he would not pull her down with him into his financial
quagmire. 'L'année 1848', he had written to his mother
from Wierzchownia, 'par des causes indépendantes de toute
volonté, me sera très lourde et difficile à passer.' He was
right. He reckoned later that the Revolution cost him
60,000 francs. The turmoil of spring and summer brought
the book-trade to a standstill: the public was in no mood for
dispassionate reading. 'Le moment est mal choisi pour faire
des romans? Faisons du théâtre.' For the rest of the year he

thought of little else, but the moment was not more favour-able to drama than the novel. Champfleury relates that he thought to organize an association of dramatists who should collaborate to furnish the Parisian theatres with plays. This was only a passing fancy.

Though his dramatic projects were numerous as usual, he had one play ready: *La Marâtre*, whose subject is a duel to the death between a woman and her step-daughter for the love of the same man. It is melodramatic, but shows more sense of the theatre than previous plays. Hostein accepted it for the Théâtre-Historique of which he was manager. It was played to half-empty houses from the 26th to the 29th of May, taken off for a time, then performed again for thirty-six nights from the 20th of July to the 26th of August. It had been well received on the first night. In *La Presse* Gautier hailed it as a new departure in drama, and even Jules Janin wrote in its favour. But the street-massacres of June kept the public out of the theatres, and thus a likely victory was snatched from Balzac's hands.

Ève disapproved of this preoccupation with the theatre, but he persisted. In August he had seventeen plays in prospect. One of them he had been preparing since 1839: *Mercadet ou le Faiseur*, a comedy in the *Turcaret* tradition showing the vices and virtues of a typical 'homme d'affaires'. It was accepted for the Théâtre-Français, newly styled the Théâtre de la République, after a very impressive reading by Balzac. But hitches occurred. Balzac went off again to Wierzchownia, and at a second reading in December the decision was reversed. Once more Balzac was frustrated when apparently on the threshold of success. He himself vetoed an unauthorized revival of *Vautrin* in April 1850. As for *Mercadet*, it was revised and revived in 1851 and ran to seventy-three performances. It has often been revived since.

Balzac's reading of *Mercadet* adds a welcome touch of the picturesque to his latter-day history. The account given by an eye-witness, the actor Edmond Got,[1] shows that even so late as 1848, when Balzac's creative energy was becoming very intermittent, he had not lost his greatest social asset: the power to amuse, astound and electrify. He came forward with his manuscript, beaming, ceremoniously attired. As he passed from act to act the effort of his mimicry was so great that he performed a kind of 'strip-tease': off went cravat, coat and waistcoat; he ended up with shirt-sleeves rolled up and buttons undone. The fact that his manuscript stopped short at the fifth act did not prevent him from declaiming it with undiminished verve and histrionic power.

He told Ève that this reading exhausted him, but there are various testimonies to the survival of the Balzacian aplomb during these months when political unrest was ruining his hopes and new symptoms of sickness were occurring. The Fourierist Jew, Alexandre Weill, who had entertained him to lunch in 1847 with Heine and Eugène Sue, records a conversation he had with him in March 1848, during which he pronounced on the political situation in his usual trenchant fashion. The novelist Champfleury, who was just beginning his career as a 'realist', had come into contact with Balzac after dedicating *Feu-Miette* to him. He visited him in March, and was entertained for three hours by this 'joyeux sanglier' who was now sporting a short beard, who boasted that only three men in France (Hugo, Gautier and himself) knew their language, and paid a characteristic compliment to Champfleury: 'Vous me ressemblez, et je suis content pour vous de cette ressemblance.'[2] The young poet Théodore de Banville sat opposite him in

[1] Reported by Jules Clarétie in *L'Opinion Nationale*, 26 Oct. 1868; quoted by Milatchitch, pp. 236–7.

[2] A. Baschet, *H. de B.* (1852), pp. 219–48.

July at a meeting of the Société des Gens de Lettres. He had not met Balzac before, but he recognized the author of the 'Comédie Humaine' in this man 'à la tête lumineuse, puissante et chevelue, éclairée par toutes les flammes de la bravoure et du génie'.[1] Auguste Vacquerie, Hugo's friend and political supporter, recalling meetings with him in July, reports that he seemed in excellent health and shows him indulging in the pipe-dream of a restored monarchy, with himself in high favour. 'Je veux une haute situation a l'étranger. J'hésite entre l'ambassade de Londres et celle de Saint-Petersbourg.'[2]

During this last exile from Ève his almost daily letters to her continued, although those subsequent to the 17th of March are not yet published. They have historical interest as a running commentary on political events. As personal missives they are true to type. They voice the agitation of his thought, his gloom about the future, his concern about the investments he and Ève had made in common. They renew for us the sad picture of Balzac the mendicant: not merely asking for money to retrieve a worsening situation (the Nord shares had fallen very low, and he wished to buy more at a cheap price), but begging for the love of which he could never for long be sure. He had good cause for uncertainty in the spring of 1848, for Ève was clearly not anxious to have him back at Wierzchownia. He tried to persuade himself—and her—that his prospects were now better than they had been in 1830 because she stood behind him. Yet melancholy phrases slipped out in which he expressed the misery of feeling that he was not really wanted. There is still some mystery about a situation which occurred in May. It looks as if Ève had tried to divert his attentions

---

[1] Banville, *Mes Souvenirs* (1888), ch. 26, p. 277.
[2] *Profils et Grimaces* (1856), pp. 229–36.

from herself by advising him to marry a young woman. At the same time Aline Moniusko, 'cette bouteille de vinaigre à deux pattes', called on him in Paris and offered him the hand of her daughter Pauline.[1] Was there collusion between Ève and Aline over so indecent a proposal? It is hard to believe that Ève could have added such insult to such injury.

It must have been a crestfallen Balzac who went in June to Saché for the last time: not to make up arrears of work as he had done in the past, but to vegetate, and to nurse the cardiac hypertrophy whose grip on him was now certain. Happily, when he got back to Paris in July he found that the pendulum had swung once more. He was to return to Wierzchownia. 'Nous allons être enfin réunis, et pour longtemps, pour le *toujours* de la terre.' Since the Revolution a sanitary cordon was drawn round Russia. He had to write letters to highly-placed officials for permission to enter the country—under strict surveillance. He entrusted the arrangement of any theatre contracts to Laurent-Jan. He left his mother to hold the fort at the 'Maison Balzac' and gave her an elaborate power-of-attorney for the management of his financial interests. He also borrowed 6,000 francs from his old publisher Souverain: he had had sundry dealings with him during the year and was to keep in touch with him by post for the next eighteen months. He left home heavily laden with clothes for a Russian winter and lamps to improve the lighting at Wierzchownia, where he must have arrived early in October.

[1] S. Collon-Bérard, 'Le dernier Voyage de B. en Russie, in *Revue de littérature comparée*, April–June 1950, p. 350, n. 5.

vii. 'Atteindre au but en expirant, comme le coureur
antique!'.[1]

He remained there until the spring of 1850. There was no
dramatic deterioration in his health until the New Year,
when he became alarmingly ill. On the 30th of April 1849
he wrote frankly to Laure about his cardiac hypertrophy,
which caused palpitations and fits of suffocation, made walk-
ing difficult, climbing impossible, and at times prevented him from even raising his arms and combing his
hair. Lung-trouble ensued in May and June, and to this
brain-fever was added in October. He was being treated by
the Wierzchownia physician, Dr Knothe, a pupil of the
famous German physician Franck. He expressed great con-
fidence in him. The treatment he received from Knothe is
described in some of his letters to Laure, to whom he wrote
more frankly than to his mother. At one stage he was taking
a course of lemon-juice which upset his stomach; at another
he was swallowing medicines and powders which Knothe
claimed as his own invention. Knothe's medical science
seems to have been little better than charlatanry, but Balzac
was pathetically grateful to him for promising a cure when
French doctors would have given him up—as Knothe's own
son, also a doctor, was inclined to do. Some idea of Knothe's
efficiency is suggested by the way he prescribed for the ar-
thritis with which Ève was afflicted:

> Tous les deux jours, elle plonge ses pieds dans un cochon de lait
> qu'on ouvre, car il faut que les pieds entrent dans les entrailles palpi-
> tantes. Il est inutile de te dire [Balzac is writing to his sister] avec
> quelle ferveur crie le petit cochon qui ne comprend pas l'honneur
> qu'on lui fait et qui voudrait s'y soustraire.[2]

A barbarous treatment, callously described. Under Knothe's

---

[1] *Albert Savarus*, Conard, iii, 81.   [2] *L. F.*, pp. 472–3.

care, Balzac continued to hope, but the attacks of heart-
trouble became more intense and prevented his return
to France. He probably had an agreeable time at Wierzchownia, at least until the end of 1848. There were moon-
light strolls in the gardens, sleigh-rides on the frozen ponds,
sometimes in the darkness, with mounted Cossacks bearing
torches to guide their way; music from the violinist; long
conversations at night by the fireside with Ève, lasting, so
runs the testimony of a Wierzchownia servant, until four
o'clock in the morning. Before long Ève's rôle as a lover must
have been exchanged for that of a sick-nurse. We should not
expect Balzac to complain to his mother or sister if Ève's
treatment of him had been unsympathetic; in fact he pays
some tributes to her kindness:

J'ai et j'aurai toujours dans Madame H. la meilleure amie, la plus
dévouée, enfin, une amie comme on n'en a qu'une dans sa vie.[1]

Anna and George were considerate, affectionate and gay:
'deux perfections idéales.' Neither of the women lacked that
nobility, common to their sex, which enabled them to support the nausea which his spittings and vomitings must have
caused them.[2]

Yet Ève still seemed determined not to marry into a
family crippled with debts. He was at pains to explain and
excuse this attitude in his letters home, and gave frequent
accounts of her money troubles. She could live comfortably
and economically at Wierzchownia on the produce of the
estates. But hard cash was not easy to come by. She only
drew (he says) 20,000 francs a year from her lands. In both
1847 and 1849 fires broke out and destroyed crops and
buildings. She had sunk fifteen years' savings into the
'Maison Balzac'. She was finding Mme Balzac's modest
personal allowance of 100 francs a month. In September

[1] *L. F.*, p. 349; 22 March 1849.   [2] Ibid., p. 494; 10 Jan. 1850.

1849 she whipped round for 20,000 francs to pay off Balzac's ancient debt to the now impoverished Mme Delannoy. The Mniszechs had their embarrassments too. Balzac blackened the picture in order to impress his mother and sister with the fact that his prospects—and consequently theirs—were still precarious. He still had to contemplate the possibility of reverting to his old life of continual labour, in as sordid conditions as those of the far-off Rue Lesdiguières. 'Il faut que je me remette à travailler,' he wrote to Fessart in September 1849, 'avec autant de persistance qu'en 1840 et 1843. . . . Soyez tranquille, il y a bien des romans dans une bouteille d'encre. . . .'[1] Alas! his efforts to write at Wierzchownia resulted only in schemes and drafts and beginnings. He must have begun to suspect, and Ève must have been fully aware, that the time was past when he could wipe out large debts by using up bottles of ink.

To this state of things we must in charity attribute the testy and ungrateful attitude that Balzac reveals in many of his letters to his mother and Laure. The former, as caretaker in the 'Maison Balzac', no doubt enjoyed such amenities as had not come her way for many years. She had also turned to piety, daily Mass, and many devotions. But he kept her busy over his affairs: money to come in and money to be paid out, and co-operation with Fessart to keep creditors out of the house—one of them, Labois, got in and seized some furniture in March 1849. Balzac was exceedingly fussy about the maintenance of the house and the completion of its furnishing. He pounced upon her for the slightest blunder or failure to execute his commissions to the letter. In March 1849, her patience gave way and she wrote him a sharp letter which caused him much humiliation. It had

[1] R. Bouvier et E. Maynial, *les Comptes dramatiques de Balzac* (Sorlot, 1938), pp. 484.

become the practice at Wierzchownia to share news in
letters at table, and Balzac started reading out this one before he realized what asperities it contained. We can imagine the tense atmosphere that reigned during the rest
of the meal—and after. Balzac was furious. The marriage
on which he had set his heart was difficult enough to
achieve without his family advertising the neediness of their
own situation (Surville as an engineer was going through a
lean period) and the disharmony of their relations. He
lashed out at his mother in a long letter which culminates
in the following reproach, prompted by the resentment he
had long felt for the favouritism she had shown in squandering her once plentiful resources on her other three children
whilst holding him strictly to his debt of 1828:

Je ne te demande certes pas de feindre des sentiments que tu
n'aurais pas, car Dieu et toi savez bien que tu ne m'as pas étouffé de
caresses ni de tendresses depuis que je suis au monde. Et tu as bien
fait, car si tu m'avais aimé comme tu as aimé Henri, je serais sans
doute où il est, et, dans ce sens, tu as été une bonne mère pour moi.
Mais ce que je voudrais, ma chère mère, *c'est l'intelligence de tes in-
térêts* que tu n'as jamais eue, c'est de ne pas barrer encore mon
avenir...[1]

He wrote the same day to Laure, imploring her to restrain
her mother from further indiscretions. The poor woman,
now over seventy-one, understood the harm she was likely
to do and became docile in the future, though never completely tactful. In September again he warned her that 'une
simple contrariété me met dans des états nerveux épouvan-
tables'. His outbursts and scoldings, and even the harsh
words quoted above, do not after all leave so bad an impression in the circumstances as the calumnies of his mother
which he had uttered in his letters to Ève on many occasions.

[1] *L. F.*, 339; 22 March 1849.

Better the forthright blow than the stab in the back. And behind the reproaches we may still discern affection for his mother. He could and did write with filial tenderness and concern, showing appreciation and gratitude for the zeal with which, henceforward, she carried out his orders. It must be remembered that the longing for marriage had for long been a monomania which coloured and warped his judgments and sapped his self-control.

Also we should remember he was now a dying man. All things were falling from him. Even his old friend and mentor Dablin was clamouring for money. We have no means of knowing the thoughts that were passing through Ève's mind during all this time. It is even possible that, in the autumn of 1849, she had him transferred to a Russian hospital for treatment of his diseases.[1]

In the first months of 1850 she was still hesitating. Then a rapid decision was made in March, and preparations were made for the wedding ceremony. There is enough evidence to show that her essential motive was pity. She knew he was doomed and resolved to give him what comfort and consolation she could during his last months of life. However much we may blame her for keeping him so long in suspense, we must recognize that this decision was a generous one. She had made a last attempt in 1849 to avoid the sacrifice of her estates, but the Tsar had remained obdurate.[2] In marrying Balzac she was condemning herself quite willingly, no doubt, to exile in Paris (for life in this city offered attractive and exciting prospects), but also to an uncertain, perhaps an impecunious future. The wedding took place at Berditcheff on the 14th of March 1850, after both Ève and Honoré had availed themselves of the sacrament of penance. His satis-

[1] W. S. Hastings, *Balzac and Souverain. An unpublished Correspondence* (New York, 1927), pp. 77–8.
[2] Korwin-Piotrowska, p. 456.

faction is revealed in the letters he immediately sent off to
his mother, Laure, the ever-faithful Nacquart, and Zulma
Carraud; it is pleasing to see that after many years of
estrangement he turned once more to this always sympathetic and affectionate friend. He was ill before and after
the ceremony, and had to linger at Wierzchownia until late
in April, when husband and wife set out on that slow, ex-
cruciating journey across the still-melting snows. Balzac had
given his mother meticulous instructions about the warming, adornment and lighting of the house in Paris. But she
must not be there to receive them. Only his manservant,
François Munsch, the Alsatian ex-soldier, whom his mother
had been told to school in the art of filling lamps, was to
await their coming. The couple arrived about the 20th of May.
He was extenuated with pain and fatigue. The house was
fully illuminated, but the doors were locked. A locksmith had
to be called in. They found Munsch inside, sitting at a table.
In the previous year Mme Balzac had expressed alarm over
his curious behaviour. He had now gone quite mad, and had
to be put in an asylum.

This nightmare was in tune with what was to follow. A
consultation between Nacquart and three other doctors, on
the 30th of May, led to the adoption of stringent, but in-
effective remedies. Balzac's eyesight was grievously affected;
he was unable to walk, and had frequent fainting-fits. Ève
settled down to her task of tending him night and day. There
is no supported evidence for the legend that she poisoned his
last weeks of life with her bad temper and cruelty. She was
gracious to his family, and her letters to Anna show distress,
as well as affection and admiration for her dying husband.
Vigny's comment—'je crois que c'est le mariage qui l'a tué'
—is both ill-informed and frivolous. There was some im-
provement in his condition in early July, when Victor Hugo

visited him and found him gay and sure of recovery. On July 11th peritonitis was diagnosed: a dubious diagnosis, says Dr Cazenove.[1] He still maintained he would live to be eighty, but by now he could no longer see to write nor hold a pen. He was still worrying over his debts, and Ève had to write his letters to Fessart. At the beginning of August he slipped and grazed his right leg on a piece of furniture. An abscess formed, then gangrene set in which an operation did not arrest. On the 18th of August he received the last sacraments and died shortly before midnight. Hugo went to see him that evening. He left (in *Choses Vues*) a restrained but sombre account of the stricken home and the unconscious man. The atmosphere in the bedroom was fetid. Only an old nurse and a manservant were keeping watch: Ève, Balzac's mother and the Surville couple had withdrawn. It is gratuitous to suppose that they did not return to see him die.

Anecdotes of Balzac's last days abound. One of the most popular, though probably spurious, is that told by Octave Mirbeau[2] about Nacquart's final visit.

'Dites-moi la vérité: où en suis-je?' . . . — 'Vous avez l'âme forte. Je vais vous dire la vérité, vous êtes perdu.' . . . — 'Ah! . . . quand dois-je mourir?' . . . — 'Vous ne passerez peut-être pas la nuit.' . . . Tout à coup, Balzac regarda longuement Nacquart et dit, dans l'intervalle de ses halètements: 'Ah! oui, je sais . . . Il me faudrait Bianchon. Bianchon me sauverait, lui!'

Bianchon is the inspired and ubiquitous doctor of the 'Comédie Humaine'; but quite frequently his task is to pronounce diseases incurable and preside over death-beds.

The funeral, a third-class one, in accordance with Balzac's own stipulation, which Ève did not find cause for revoking, took place at the parish church, Saint-Philippe du Roule, on

---

[1] *Le Drame de B.*, p. 72, n. i. Cf. above, p. 128–9.
[2] 'La mort de Balzac', in *Bords du Rhin, Récits de voyage*, 1907.

the 21st of August. The body was buried at Père-Lachaise. The Minister of the Interior was present, and representatives of learned and august societies like the French Academy, to which Balzac had several times demanded admission, but in vain. A large concourse of public men, writers and artists also attended, Sainte-Beuve among them. Balzac's other inveterate foe, Jules Janin, had become friendly of late. According to Julien Lemer, he was not present at the funeral, but paid him a resounding tribute that evening, at a bankers' dinner. Hugo's speech at the grave-side was worthy, both of himself and the colleague whose death he mourned. 'M. de Balzac était un des premiers parmi les plus grands, un des plus hauts parmi les meilleurs. . . . A son insu, qu'il le veuille ou non, l'auteur de cette œuvre immense et étrange est de la forte race des écrivains révolutionnaires.' Hugo was a man whom Balzac sometimes suspected, sometimes disparaged, and sometimes despised. I believe there is no record of Hugo having ever spoken or written of Balzac with anything but respect and admiration.[1] The same is true of Lamartine.

Two things remained behind: debts and the 'Comédie Humaine'. To say that Mme de Balzac paid for the former with the latter would be too bald a statement. He left assets valued at 169,240 francs; he owed 83,502 francs at his death, including the 13,000 francs which were still due to his mother, and which, according to the terms of his will, were to be repaid in the form of an annuity of 3,000 francs. Mme de Balzac had paid out to him or for him, including the *trésor louloup*, nigh on 400,000 francs. Her means were now appreciably reduced. She gave the famous walking-

[1] For letters that passed between the two writers, see R. Pierrot, 'Balzac et Hugo d'après leur correspondance', *Revue d'histoire littéraire*, Oct.–Dec. 1953. See also J. B. Barrère, 'Hugo jaugé par Balzac', *Mercure de France*, 1 Jan. 1950.

stick to Dr Nacquart, and accepted the responsibility of paying the stipulated annuity to her mother-in-law, who lived on for nearly four more years. In the meantime she set to work to pay off the rest of her husband's obligations by finishing the publication of his works and arranging new editions. It is fair to state that she did this for his glory as well as for her own benefit. She began this exploitation with the aid of Dutacq and Champfleury and then with that of the third-rate novelist Charles Rabou.

She mourned for her husband. At first she wrote of following him to a better world: this mood did not last. She gave herself in succession to two other men, Champfleury and the painter, Jean Gigoux. She died in 1882.

Indignation against Ève and sentimentality in her favour are equally pointless. Balzac was an exceptional man, and beyond her power to measure. It is not easy to imagine how the pattern of his life would have developed had they never met; it is permissible to regret that they ever did meet.

V

THE ESSENTIAL BALZAC

L'artiste, selon moi, est une monstruosité,
quelque-chose hors nature. Tous les mal-
heurs dont la Providence l'accable lui vien-
nent de l'entêtement qu'il a à nier cet axiome.
Gustave Flaubert.

i. Balzac as seen by his contemporaries

'LE DERNIER ACTE est sanglant, quelque belle que soit la
comédie en tout le reste.' To judge by the *Lettres à l'Étran-*
gère, neither the middle nor the later scenes of the Balzac
comedy were remarkable for their beauty. But the *Lettres*
give only one aspect: Balzac as drudge, adding-machine,
yearning, frustrated lover. A very different Balzac claims
our attention, the gay, ardent, mercurial, irrepressible spirit
who springs to life again from the pages of those who knew
him.

Not that many of them were able to keep him in sight
for long stretches at a time. He was an elusive person, disappearing for weeks and months, reappearing and taking up
relationships as if they had never been interrupted. When
he did reappear, he was so vivid and vital that his friends,
Nacquart excepted, never thought of him wearing out and
disappearing for ever. In June 1850, on the eve of a journey
to Italy, Théophile Gautier called at the Rue Fortunée and
found no-one at home. Balzac had slipped his leash and gone
out against doctor's orders. He was none the less so ill that
his wife had to write the letter in which he expressed his
regret for having missed Gautier; but he managed to scrawl

a line at the bottom of the page: 'Je ne puis ni lire, ni écrire.'
Yet Gautier was not alarmed. 'L'idée que Balzac pût mourir
ne nous vint seulement pas.' His supply of animal spirits
seemed inexhaustible, his zest for life unquenchable.

What did he look like? Here is the Balzac one might have
glimpsed in the streets of Paris any day in 1838, according
to Paul Lacroix:

> . . . un petit homme ventru, à la bouche vermeille, aux yeux vifs et
> perçants, à la physionomie ouverte et joyeuse, à la démarche lourde et
> insouciante; . . . admirable tête de génie; corps épais de commis
> voyageur; chapeau à larges bords, chauve et poudreux; redingote
> noire, râpée partout et blanche aux coutures; cravate roulée en corde
> autour du cou; bottes éculées et grimaçantes.[1]

Gautier gives an indoor view of him as he knew him in
1835. It is an indispensable portrait:

> Son froc rejeté en arrière laissait à découvert son col d'athlète ou de
> taureau, rond comme un tronçon de colonne, sans muscles apparents
> et d'une blancheur satinée qui contrastait avec le ton plus coloré de la
> face. . . . Son pur sang tourangeau fouettait ses joues pleines d'un
> pourpre vivace et coloriait chaudement ses bonnes lèvres épaisses et
> sinueuses, faciles au rire; de légères moustaches et une mouche en
> accentuaient les contours sans les cacher; le nez, carré du bout, par-
> tagé en deux lobes, coupé de narines bien ouvertes, avait un caractère
> tout à fait original et particulier; aussi Balzac, en posant pour son
> buste, le recommandait-il à David d'Angers: 'Prenez garde à mon nez;
> — mon nez, c'est un monde!' Le front était beau, vaste, noble, sensible-
> ment plus blanc que le masque, sans autre pli qu'un sillon perpendicu-
> laire à la racine du nez; les protubérances de la mémoire des lieux
> formaient une saillie très prononcée au-dessus des arcades sourcilières;
> les cheveux abondants, longs, durs, et noirs, se rebroussaient en arrière
> comme une crinière léonine. Quant aux yeux, il n'en exista jamais de
> pareils. Ils avaient une vie, une lumière, un magnétisme inconcevables
> . . . la sclérotique en était pure, limpide, bleuâtre, comme celle d'un
> enfant ou d'une vierge, et enchâssait deux diamants noirs qu'éclairaient
> par instants de riches reflets d'or; c'étaient des yeux à faire baisser la

[1] Quoted in Lovenjoul, *H. O.*, p. 473.

prunelle aux aigles, à lire à travers les murs et les poitrines, à foud-
royer une bête fauve furieuse, des yeux de souverain, de voyant, de
dompteur. . . .

Ces yeux extraordinaires, dès qu'on avait rencontré leur regard, em-
pêchaient de remarquer ce que les autres traits pouvaient présenter
de trivial ou d'irrégulier.

L'expression habituelle de la figure était une sorte d'hilarité puissante, de joie rabelaisienne et monacale — le froc contribuait sans
doute à faire naître cette idée — qui vous faisaient penser à frère Jean
des Entommeures, mais agrandi et relevé par un esprit de premier
ordre . . . ses mains . . . étaient d'une beauté rare, de vraies mains de
prélat, blanches, aux doigts menus et potelés, aux ongles roses et bril-
lants; il en avait la coquetterie et souriait de plaisir quand on les re-
gardait.[1]

It looks as if Gautier, while recalling these first-hand im-
pressions, had Boulanger's portrait of 1837 in mind. Elsewhere he has analyzed the portrait itself. But his description
certainly hits off the original in his essential features. Other
verbal portraits, whether friendly or hostile, confirm most of
the details, as do the numerous drawings and caricatures
which Balzac inspired.[2] Even the malevolent Lambinet,[3]
trying to make Balzac as grotesque and unsavoury as possible, gives virtual corroboration. He adds that Balzac's
hair was unkempt and greasy, and other accounts prove
that this was often so. His eyes, says Lambinet, 'auraient
été superbes, sans leur expression inquisitoriale, effrontée et
cynique.' His finger-nails were black until he took to gnaw-
ing them. Lambinet also exaggerates his corpulence as well
as the awkwardness of his figure and gait.

This ungainliness, which is well-vouched for, is only

[1] Th. Gautier, *H. de Balzac*, 1858. The quotations are from Boschot's
edition of *Souvenirs romantiques*, 1929, 107–10.
[2] See below, Appendix, *Notes on the Iconography of Balzac*. He often
gave idealized portraits of himself in his novels. Gautier vouches for the
fidelity of the self-portrait in the description of Albert Savarus.
[3] *Balzac mis à nu*, 26–7.

hinted at by the kindly Gautier. He says nothing about his teeth, which were decayed and discoloured. Vigny, who clearly disliked him on first acquaintance, deprives him of his upper set in 1827, but remarks upon the whiteness and completeness of his teeth in 1844.[1] Had Balzac bought a false set by then? Nothing in his correspondence supports this conjecture, though he writes much of teeth trouble in later years. All eye-witnesses are agreed about the fiery, penetrating glance, while Lamartine, describing the Balzac he met and admired in 1833, discerns a confidential friendliness in it.

There is abundant testimony about two facts; the general vulgarity of his appearance and his lack of personal fastidiousness. His sincerest admirers, captivated by the spiritual qualities shining through the grossness of the exterior, are content to hint at this. The snobs speak plainly—Fontaney, Delacroix, Rodolphe Apponyi, the Countess de Bassanville, Eusèbe de Sales, Gavarni; even Léon Gozlan joins this chorus. 'Figure de panetier, tournure de savetier, envergure de tonnelier, allure de bonnetier, mine de cabaretier' wrote the supercilious Hector de Balabine when he met him in St. Petersburg in 1843.[2] Nor can it be doubted that he was shabby, unshaven, slovenly and often dirty except when attired for social occasions; he then overdressed and used too much pomade and perfume.

Those who listened to him, in drawing-room or by the fireside, forgot these blemishes, so entrancing was his discourse. Not that he was a fine wit, brilliant in repartee or subtle in epigram. The examples which he gives, in some of his *Scènes*, of what he considers to be scintillating talk show how far he must have fallen short in this respect.

[1] Letter to the Vicomtesse du Plessis, 15 Sept. 1850. See Vigny's *Correspondance, 1816–1863* (Calmann-Lévy, 1905, pp. 191–4).

[2] Quoted by Billy, *Vie de Balzac*, ii, 115.

Although, as a rule, he was not inclined to share much in general conversation, there were times when, probably through embarrassment, he talked too much of himself. He was at his best when the company deferred to him and let dialogue dwindle into monologue.

Tantôt, says Lamartine, il se baissait jusqu'à terre comme pour ramasser une gerbe d'idées, tantôt il se redressait sur la pointe des pieds pour suivre le vol de sa pensée jusqu'à l'infini. . . . Ses bras gesticulaient avec aisance; il causait comme un orateur parle. Sa voix était retentissante de l'énergie un peu sauvage de ses poumons, mais elle n'avait ni rudesse, ni ironie, ni colère. Cette parlante figure, dont on ne pouvait détacher ses regards, vous charmait et vous fascinait.[1]

So it was in 1833. So it had been in 1828, when Balzac more than paid for his keep at Fougères by entertaining his hosts with tales made up on the spur of the moment—*du Balzac tout pur*, as he gleefully admitted to his audience. So it was, right into the late forties, as is proved by the eagerness of Delphine de Girardin to entice him to her gatherings of distinguished people. When in congenial surroundings he was loquacious, inventive and captivating. No-one knew better than Delphine how to draw him out, and Gautier wrote pages on the fascination which Balzac exerted over his hearers once he began to spin his tales. Delighted with his own gift as an improviser, bursting with laughter at his own sallies, he carried his listeners with him even when they were inclined to feel shocked at the raciness or audacity of his 'jovialité herculéenne'.

Ne croyez pas cependant que Balzac cherchait à divertir sa galerie! Il obéissait à une sorte d'ivresse intérieure et peignait en traits rapides, avec une intensité comique et un talent bouffe incomparables, les fantasmagories bizarres qui dansaient dans la chambre noire de son cerveau.[2]

[1] Lamartine, *Cours familier de littérature*, vol. 18: *Balzac et ses œuvres*, pp. 16–17.
[2] *Souvenirs romantiques*, p. 151.

Balzac's laughter was boisterous and contagious. The word 'Rabelaisian' unfailingly recurs both in personal descriptions and in accounts of his talent as a raconteur and a reader.[1] But he had more than entertainment value. Many people testify to a more fundamental attractiveness.

Il y avait, Mme de Pommereul said of her 1828 guest, dans tout son ensemble, dans ses gestes, dans sa manière de parler, de se tenir, tant de confiance, tant de bonté, tant de naïveté, tant de franchise, qu'il était impossible de le connaître sans l'aimer.[2]

To his generous and sympathetic portrait of Balzac, Lamartine adds:

Le trait dominant du visage était, plus même que l'intelligence, la bonté communicative. Il vous ravissait l'esprit quand il parlait; même en se taisant, il vous ravissait le cœur. Aucune passion de haine ou d'envie n'aurait pu être exprimée par cette physionomie; il lui aurait été impossible de n'être pas bon. . . . Un enfantillage réjoui, c'était le caractère de cette figure; une âme en vacances quand il laissait la plume pour s'oublier avec ses amis.[3]

George Sand, who knew him far better than Lamartine, strikes a similar note:

Puéril et puissant, toujours curieux d'un *bibelot*, et jamais jaloux d'une gloire, sincère jusqu'à la modestie, vantard jusqu'à la hâblerie, confiant en lui-même et aux autres, très-expansif, très-bon et très-fou, avec un sanctuaire de raison intérieure, où il rentrait pour tout dominer dans son œuvre, cynique dans la chasteté, ivre en buvant de l'eau, intempérant de travail et sobre d'autres passions, positif et romanesque avec un égal excès, crédule et sceptique, plein de contrastes et de mystères, tel était Balzac encore jeune. . . . Son âme était d'une grande sérénité, et en aucun moment je ne l'ai vu maussade.[4]

These testimonies, in which stress is laid on Balzac's goodness of heart, are early ones. George Sand is thinking mainly

[1] See above, ch. iv, p. 120.
[2] Quoted by Ét. Aubrée, *Balzac à Fougères* (Librairie académique Perrin, 1939), p. 94.
[3] Op. cit., pp. 16–17.   [4] *Hist. de ma vie*, 1856, t. 9, 15.

of what he was like in 1831, although she had enough to do with him throughout his later career to have revised her judgment had she seen fit. Other and later testimonies are not quite so unanimous. But the contrasts and paradoxes which George Sand brings out are confirmed by evidence from various sources. There is no doubt for instance about his vanity and boastfulness. *Ah! que c'est beau!* he is reported to have exclaimed during a pause in his reading of one of his novels at a literary soirée. He was delighted at any sign of adulation, proud of his European reputation, thought of himself as the Napoleon of letters, and at times his opinion of himself did not fall far short of megalomania.

He was spontaneously egotistical. He tried to use his friends, Gozlan, Lassailly, Laurent-Jan and even Gautier, for the furtherance of his own literary projects and, in his one-sided conversations with most of them, exhausted them by his exuberance and restlessness. He was so absorbed in his own creations that he readily brushed aside other people's talk of theirs, or of ordinary human matters. 'Allons, disait-il, c'est très bien, mais revenons à la réalité . . . que ferons-nous de Nucingen, de la duchesse de Langeais?'[1] On the other hand, what Laure Surville called his 'naïf enthousiasme de lui-même' alternated with moods of anxiety and doubts about the value of his works. Perhaps he never really welcomed criticism, but when it was sincere he was capable of pondering over it and correcting the defects indicated. 'Souvent', says Victor Ratier, 'je l'ai vu déchirer avec des larmes de désespoir des pages que, la veille, il avait proclamées admirables.'[2] His obstinacy in proof-correction shows a perpetual dissatisfaction, and he was particularly sensitive about the imperfections of his style.

[1] Sainte-Beuve, *Nouveaux Lundis*, viii, 110.
[2] Quoted by Lovenjoul, *H. O.*, 403.

His amiability towards others was not always in evidence. He could be self-assertive to the point of brutality in dealing with editors, critics and creditors. If we are to believe Werdet, he could be insolently cruel to literary neophytes like Jules Bergounioux, a young contributor to the *Chronique de Paris* on whom he pounced one day for presuming to compare himself with 'the marshals of modern literature'. Over against this we can set the friendly counsel he gave to other young writers—Lemer in 1838 and Champfleury in 1848. He could be impulsively generous. He was so to Werdet himself, in the intervals of wheedling money out of him, and to two young friends whose rooms he once decided to redecorate as a pleasant surprise. It is true that he spoilt this gesture by neglecting to pay for the cost of it; but Werdet, although his *Portrait Intime* bears unmistakable signs of the grievance he nursed against Balzac, gives him credit for many genuine acts of kindness, especially to his own servants, Auguste Depril, Rose, and his 'tiger' Grain de Mil. In short he discerns a contrast between 'l'homme bon, généreux, au cœur d'or, tel que le Créateur l'avait formé' and 'l'homme égoïste . . . qui s'était corrompu au contact du monde'.

That this goodness of heart should have suffered some diminution as middle age advanced and the struggle for life became harder is, alas, only too human and natural. We have seen from his letters to Mme Hanska and his mother that he could be harsh, vindictive and disloyal. His gratitude to benefactors, even Dablin, Mme Delannoy, Buisson and Mme Guidoboni-Visconti, was subject to intermittence. The reasons for such deterioration have been made clear, but there is proof that through illness and tribulation the fundamental Balzac persisted. We should do him an injustice by supposing that during his last years he was a soured and disgruntled man, incapable of rising superior to his own sorrows. His letters to his nieces, Sophie and Valentine Surville, during his second sojourn at Wierzchownia, give an agreeable impression of him as a benevolent and affectionate uncle. Ève herself pays a great tribute to him in a letter of April 1850.

Je ne me faisais pas l'idée de ce que c'est que cet adorable être, je le connaissais depuis 17 ans et tous les jours je m'aperçois qu'il y a une qualité nouvelle que je ne lui connaissais pas.[1]

In April and May 1850 Anna Mniszech was writing letters to her mother in Paris. They are full of tender references to and messages for 'Bilboquet'. Far from grudgingly accepting him as an intruder between her mother and herself, she enthusiastically adopted him as a 'Père adoré'.[2]

ii. The legendary Balzac

The picture of Balzac would be far from complete if no account were taken of his eccentricity, his antics and his escapades, a constant source of surprise and amusement to his friends and acquaintances. From their reminiscences the legendary Balzac has emerged. He himself did a great deal to create this unconventional figure: unconsciously, for he was made like that; and deliberately too, for he was not blind to the advantages of publicity. He probably enjoyed reading such nonsense as P. L. Jacob wrote about him in 1838:

... on assure que M. de Balzac ne joue de la plume qu'en présence de trois cent soixante-quinze portraits de femmes adorables ou du moins adorées; on dit que son appartement, sombre et mystérieux comme une alcôve, tout parfumé de fleurs et de cassolettes, est rempli de chiffres entrelacés, de tendres devises, de monuments votifs, de cœurs embaumés, venus des quatre parties du monde; on dit que le grand pontife

[1] M. Bouteron, *La véritable image de Mme Hanska*, 31.
[2] Korwin-Piotrowska, op. cit., 460–4.

177

de ce sanctuaire ne vit que d'opium et de bétel, ne dort que sur des feuilles de rose, ne compose que dans des bains odoriférants; on dit encore que M. de Balzac, qui emploie pour son habillement plus d'aunes de soie et de dentelles que Rabelais n'en a fait entrer dans le costume de Gargantua, est si sensible d'épiderme et si délicat pour le choix de son linge, qu'il s'est fait fabriquer des chemises avec des toiles d'araignées et des *fils de la bonne Vierge*; on dit enfin que ce sybarite raffiné est entouré d'une foule d'esclaves, qui se prosternent la face contre la terre lorsqu'il éternue, et qui allument son narguillet [*sic*] avec des billets de la Banque de France. . . .[1]

His daily habits have become part of the legend. Enough has already been said of his working time-table and his curious method of composition and correction. These, and everything else about him, have the cachet of abnormality. His way of life swings from one extreme to the other: at one moment the cheerful acceptance of discomfort and deprivation, at another the expansive indulgence of sybaritic tastes. His eating habits exhibit the same contrast. While he was immersed in work his meals were frugal in the literal sense of the word——he was fond of pears and peaches. Then came the monster repasts which, during his periods of relaxation, he took himself or served to his friends. Werdet has given the account of one of these.[2] Alfred de Nettement describes another, which Balzac offered to him and other writers recruited in 1835 for the *Chronique de Paris*: a sequence of oysters and cutlets repeated so many times that for three months afterwards Nettement declares himself to have been unable to look a basket of oysters in the face.[3]

Normally Balzac drank little wine, for he lived in a continuous state of 'ivresse intérieure'; but he could empty four bottles of Vouvray without turning a hair. He had a preju-

---

[1] *Le Constitutionnel*, 30 Sept. 1838.   [2] See above, ch. iii, p. 72.
[3] M. Bouteron, *Une année de la vie de Balzac* (Monaco, 1925), p. 47.

dice against certain stimulants, and wrote against them in
the *Traité des excitants modernes* (1838). Tobacco he loathed,
though George Sand did once persuade him to take some
puffs at a hookah; whereupon he asked Mme Hanska to send
him a narghile and some latakia, but the whim soon passed.
He tells how a single cigar once made him drunk, an effect
which large libations of wine could never produce. The idea
of surrendering his intelligence to the influence of hashish
was repugnant to him, though Gautier once induced him to
make a half-hearted trial of it.

As is well known, he drank coffee to excess. He professed
to be a connoisseur of tea. But even in these routine indul-
gences fantasy played its part. His coffee must be of a special
blend, and he must needs parade the fact by dragging
Gozlan all over Paris to buy the different berries. His tea,
by his own account—as reported by Gozlan—came from a
supply graciously presented to the Emperor of Russia by the
Emperor of China, after the plants had been tended by the
most exalted mandarins, and the leaves plucked before dawn
by maidens who bore it with song to the Emperor's feet. The
quite ordinary wines with which he regaled his friends were
transformed, by a stroke of imagination, into wonderful
beverages with a romantic history behind them.

In short, Balzac could not resist the urge to bathe his
everyday life in a Thousand-and-one-Nights atmosphere.
Hence the many absurdities that are related of him. Their
flavour is dulled if the trimmings are left out, but a few of
them may be briefly recalled here. Grateful for services
rendered, he presses on Latouche the gift of an Arab horse,
is outraged when he refuses such an inconvenient gift, and
supremely satisfied when, for the sake of peace and quiet, he
accepts. It goes without saying that Latouche never had to
face the problem of finding a stable for this non-existent

animal.[1]—Balzac speeds across Paris to wake Laurent-Jan up at two in the morning, and wants him to set out immediately, with himself and Gozlan, for the Empire of the Grand Mogul. He has learned that the *bedouck* ring, given him in Vienna by the Baron von Hammer-Purgstall, is the long-lost ring of the Prophet, stolen a century ago from the Grand Mogul. Tons of gold and diamonds will be theirs if they restore it to that potentate.—Balzac dines Gustave Planche (at Buisson's expense) in Véry's restaurant, and in the course of a sumptuous dinner offers his guest a choice of brilliant appointments:

'Voulez-vous l'ambassade de Constantinople? criait-il à Planche en le tirant par les boutons de son habit. 'Le ministère de l'Instruction publique vous irait peut-être mieux? Malheureusement j'y ai mis quelqu'un. Nous arrangerons ça. Il me reste l'Espagne, vous n'en voulez pas?' 'Je ne dis pas non', répondit Planche.[2]

The repertory of anecdotes is inexhaustible. Many of them are apocryphal, many richly embroidered. Are the authentic ones to be explained as the hallucinations of a half-crazy genius? Are they the calculated gestures of a practical joker intent on self-advertisement—*du Balzac tout pur!* he may sometimes have said to himself as he savoured the stupefaction of his dupes. Or are they the *galéjades* of a grown-up schoolboy letting off steam?

The schoolboy is often enough to the fore. He presides as Grand-Master over the meetings and conspiratorial secrecy of the Order of the Cheval Rouge. He leads the team of cronies who tiptoe forth at night from Les Jardies to push down, with iron-shod sticks, the loose-stone wall of an

---

[1] Sainte-Beuve told this story in 1834 (*Portraits contemporains*, II, p. 342, note), Werdet (*Portrait intime*, pp. 138–140) puts the anecdote later, and names Jules Sandeau as the person for whom this unsubstantial present was destined.

[2] Jules Vallès, *Les Réfractaires* (1863)—'Un Réfractaire illustre'.

obnoxious neighbour. No doubt it is the practical joker—
though debts and distraint are not so funny—who devises
the plan for reducing Les Jardies, servants, guests and watch-
dog, to rigid immobility and silence when a creditor rings
the bell: *Mais ils sont donc tous morts là-dedans!* And, however genuine may be Balzac's celebrated whimsy about the
mysterious correspondence existing between men's names
and the destiny reserved for them, surely the practical joker
is not entirely absent when Gozlan is haled round Paris,
scanning innumerable shop-signs, until the significant pat-
ronymic of MARCAS is lighted on!

On the other hand, Balzac's gravity cannot be questioned
when it comes to the invention of schemes for rapid enrichment. He really did think of himself as a shrewd businessman and an inspired financier. Scarcely a year passed by
without some ingenious project occurring to him. His ideas
are not all far-fetched. The 'Société d'Abonnement générale',
for instance, which he had in mind from 1831 to 1833, was
a plan for the cheap publication of books. Its success would
depend on finding the right kind of paper and getting a
large number of subscribers. For the sum of 120 francs a
year each subscriber would receive, every month, eight
volumes of history or fiction. A similar project, conceived in
1837, was less practicable: an illustrated edition of his works
was to be published with an additional attraction offered to
subscribers: an interest in a tontine and the chance of winning an annuity of 30,000 francs. In 1848, when the difficulty of inducing the public to buy books was increased by
the hazards of revolution, the Librairie Universelle devised
a similar but less ambitious scheme, that of offering lottery
tickets to purchasers. It is no matter for surprise that Balzac
joined in the gamble and commissioned Souverain to buy
him some of the books. In the meantime his brain had been

fertile in other speculative projects. To the Sardinian mines affair, the Monceaux land-speculation and the plan for importing timber from the Ukraine may be added the idea he (or Surville) had in 1836 of a canal to be cut from Nantes to Orléans. The drawback to this was that a capital of 26 million francs would be needed.

The Balzac who imagines such ventures is certainly the Balzac who has an eye to the main chance, who revolutionizes the novel by giving primary importance to the acquisitive instinct, who makes all the money he can from the exploitation of his works, plays a game of tug-of-war with publishers and editors, and tries, by flattery and rich fare (with his plate redeemed from pawn for the occasion), to persuade a reputedly wealthy greenhorn to invest in the *Chronique de Paris*. But even where financial speculation is concerned there is always a likelihood of the dreamer or the *halluciné* taking charge. He does so when Balzac reveals to Gautier his plan for growing pineapples in the allegedly sun-drenched grounds of Les Jardies and buying a shop in Paris in order to sell them and thus reap a profit of 400,000 francs per annum. It is the dreamer who proposes to buy a blue rose and win a horticultural prize of half a million francs; who claims that the walnut-tree on his estate will bring him a steady income because all the local inhabitants are obliged by custom to shoot their rubbish underneath it and so provide him with a rich supply of manure—*C'est du guano!* It is especially at moments of disappointment that such fantastic schemes crowd into the brain of this Baron von Münchhausen. After the failure of *Vautrin* he consoled himself with the thought of buying pedigree cattle and starting a dairy, or of setting up as a market-gardener and selling rare vegetables to rich consumers—for a total annual profit of 6,000 francs. His friends listened to these calcula-

tions with amused incredulity, but sometimes they pricked
the bubble with unkind promptitude. The story runs that
one day Henri Monnier, after hearing Balzac totting up the
score of millions to be gained from the mass-production of
plays at the Porte Saint-Martin theatre, held his hand out
and said: 'Avance-moi cent sous sur l'affaire.'

Whatever their motive and occasion may be, these tara-
diddles seem to show that Balzac, in his waking life, still
hovered on the brink of the dream-world which he inhabited as author of the 'Comédie Humaine'. In all probability, a large part of his eccentricity results from the
superimposition of this dream-world on the world of reality.
Perhaps also a large part of his superstition may be explained in the same way, especially at those times when this
admirer of fortune-tellers claimed to work miracles by the
laying-on of hands and offered to magnetize his future wife
so that she might travel in comfort in spite of pregnancy.
It has indeed been maintained that Balzac's fictitious world
was more real to him, or at any rate, more important, than
the one he stepped into after his long wrestling bouts with
the demon of inspiration. He could retire into it anew,
as into a sure refuge, whenever financial and sentimental
worries were too great; and not even Mme Hanska could
follow him there. Without her, his debts would not have
troubled him much. Under pressure from her, they troubled
him a great deal. The remedy was to plunge back into his
work, when work was possible, and so long as the tyranny of
external events did not wring from his lips the cry of despair:
je fais du Sue tout pur! So that the labour over which he
groaned was in fact the labour for which, in his heart of
hearts, he longed.

Is this too much of a paradox? Certainly we should
not carry it so far as to be able only to see Balzac as a phan-

tasmagoric figure for ever brooding over his phantasma-
goric creation, like a ghostly Napoleon eternally holding his
ghostly armies in review. Balzac was of the real world, loved
it, and modelled his fictitious world on it. But at his desk,
with his paper and raven's quill before him, he is the master
of both these worlds, at once the dispenser of visions and the
discoverer of his own age. At his desk, this man whom
Brunetière upbraids for thinking only of success and money,
this 'immense bonhomme' whom Flaubert accuses of having
too little love for art, no doubt recaptures that 'serenity'
which George Sand found in him. It descends upon him and
envelops him as the children of Israel were enveloped by
the cloud which hid them from their foes.

APPENDIX

Notes on the Iconography of Balzac

Portraits and caricatures of Balzac abound. Many of them are assembled in the work of Pierre Abraham: *Balzac, Recherches sur la création intellectuelle*, Rieder, 1929. A wider selection appears in *Encyclopédie par l'Image: Balzac*, Hachette, 1950. Here are listed those which the verbal descriptions quoted in Chapter V most fully corroborate.

PORTRAITS

1821. A sepia drawing attributed to Achille Devéria. An eager, bright-eyed, intelligent young man, with a touch of feminine beauty. Abraham, Plate I.

1829 (*circa*). A sepia drawing by Louis Boulanger. A pose of cheerful self-confidence and purposefulness. Abraham, Plate XXI.

1836. A lithograph by Julien published in *Le Voleur*. Plump face, resolute chin. Shows amiability, intelligence, strength. Abraham, Plate VII.

1836. A portrait by Boulanger, sent to Wierzchownia and badly preserved. Described by Gautier in his 'Salon de 1837' (*La Presse*, 6 Dec., 1836). Balzac in his monachal robe, with arms folded. Brilliant eyes, sensuality and humour in the mouth, a swelling chin. Abraham, Plate XIII.

1842. Daguerreotype by Nadar. Balzac in shirt-sleeves, with left hand folded across his chest in a favourite Napoleonic attitude. Face somewhat bloated, but shows energy and self-confidence: the face and poise of a man who is hard-driven but determined. Lovenjoul regarded this as the most faithful likeness of Balzac. See Frontispiece.

1843. Sketch by David d'Angers for the bust he was making. Head in profile. The traditional mane of hair. Clear-cut features ('tête olympienne', wrote Balzac to Mme Hanska, *E*, ii, 220). Proud, confident poise. Brings out the length of the nose on its broad base, and the firmness of the chin as admitted by Lambinet, though there is a fold of fat under it. Laure Surville regarded this as the best drawing of her brother. Abraham, Plate XXV.

1847. A black-lead drawing by Bertall, engraved on steel for the Furne-Houssiaux continuation of the 'Comédie Humaine'. In the monk's robe. Face rather bloated, but brings out resolution and humour. Abraham, Plate XVII.

CARICATURES

The aim of caricature is of course to exaggerate conspicuous traits. The most justly renowned caricatures are as follows:

1835. Statuette by Dantan. Balzac as dandy, with top-hat and cane. The features over-emphasized are the cane, the grin on the face and the corpulence. Abraham, Plate X.

1838. By Benjamin Roubaud for *La Caricature*. Balzac in his monk's robe with long hair falling over his shoulders, Rabelaisian grin (showing bad teeth), fat cheeks and double chin. Itself a caricature of the Boulanger portrait. Balzac in his turn did a crayon drawing of it in the album of Countess Bolognini (later Princesse Porcia). Abraham, Plate XVI.

1839. *Balzac aux Tuileries*, by Cassal. Of no value at all for Balzac's physiognomy, but it shows Balzac in his smartest get-up. Really neither a portrait nor a caricature. *Encyclopédie par l'Image, Balzac*, 24.

1843. Balzac riding a hobby-horse and brandishing a sword, surrounded by journalists. Done by J. Platier for *La Mode*, apropos of *Monographie de la presse parisienne*.

It brings out his corpulence and his gleeful vigour in castigating his enemies. Abraham, Plate XVIII.

The two group-caricatures following are of small value
for the iconography of Balzac, but they show him in the
company of celebrities of the time:

1843. 'Le Thé chez Mme de Girardin.' By Grandville in
L. Reybaud's *Jérôme Paturot à la recherche d'une position
sociale.* Abraham, Plate XII. The reproduction in *Encyclopédie par l'Image*, p. 21, is better.

1843. 'Grand Chemin de la Postérité.' By Benjamin
Roubaud. A crowd of literary stars of the period, marching
towards hoped-for fame. Abraham, Plate XXVIII.

STATUES

David d'Angers' bust of 1844 is the most famous. It brings
out the strength of the face enclosed in the mane of hair,
but all vitality is lost through the eyes being closed. Abraham, Plate XXIII.

Puttinati's statuette of 1837 is of no value for the face.
Abraham, Plate XI.

The commissioned statue by Falguière (1899) makes an
Apollo of Balzac. *Encyclopédie par l'Image*, p. 48.

The controversial twentieth-century statue by Rodin
gives him the appearance of a rugged, tortured, emaciated
Titan. It expresses strength and achievement through
suffering. Abraham, Plate XXXVII.

Rodin's bronze head of Balzac is more like him, but still
shows him grim and tormented. Abraham, Plate LX.

INDEX